Gabriel's Journey

By

Thomas J. Prestopnik

ISBN: 1-4107-3589-3 (e-book)
ISBN: 1-4107-3587-7 (Paperback)
ISBN: 1-4107-3588-5 (Hardcover)

Library of Congress Control Number: 2003092006

This book is printed on acid free paper.

Printed in the United States of America
Bloomington, IN

1stBooks – rev. 04/12/03

CONTENTS

CHAPTER ONE
The Storm 1

CHAPTER TWO
News From Across the Road 3

CHAPTER THREE
Warning Signs 11

CHAPTER FOUR
The Search Begins 16

CHAPTER FIVE
Finding A Friend.. 24

CHAPTER SIX
A Possible Solution.. 30

CHAPTER SEVEN
The Debate.. 39

CHAPTER EIGHT
Sleepwalking.. 46

CHAPTER NINE
A Gathering Of Frogs 53

CHAPTER TEN
Betrayal.. 64

CHAPTER ELEVEN
The Journey Begins 67

CHAPTER TWELVE
The Final Stretch.. 82

CHAPTER THIRTEEN
   A New Home 90

CHAPTER FOURTEEN
   Explorations 95

CHAPTER FIFTEEN
   The Wall 102

CHAPTER SIXTEEN
   Lights, Tents, Tables and Chairs 107

CHAPTER SEVENTEEN
   The Trouble With Simon 113

CHAPTER EIGHTEEN
   The Big Day 119

CHAPTER NINETEEN
   Hide and Seek 135

CHAPTER TWENTY
   Weather and Time 150

CHAPTER TWENTY-ONE
   Another Journey 156

For Dad,
Who now watches over us.

John W. Prestopnik
(1924-2002)

GABRIEL'S FIELD

Illustrated by Thomas J. Prestopnik

CHAPTER ONE

The Storm

It swooped down upon the countryside with the speed of an eagle, charged like an angry bull, then savagely attacked with a lion's lethal fury. There had never been a summer storm quite like it.

Lightning seared the midnight sky as thunder rocked the ground like dynamite. Cold rain fell in gray sheets, ripped to shreds by the howling bitter wind. A mass of billowing black clouds rolled in from the west and settled over the field while sharp winds twisted tall grass into tangles and snapped off tree limbs in the nearby woods.

Just below the surface, in a scattering of holes and small tunnels, the field mice rolled themselves into snug furry bundles to ward off the night's violent frenzy. None of their tiny eyes saw what happened next.

A lightning flash sliced through the raucous clouds. It struck an abandoned barn across the road from the mice's field and blasted the rooftop to bits. The wood burst into flames that quickly engulfed the walls and rafters. Glowing timbers hissed and sputtered as grape-size raindrops pelted the earth. Forked flames, glowing yellow and orange, snapped at the air like snake tongues.

1

A wailing chorus erupted from inside the burning blackness, followed by a riot of scratching claws and glowing green eyes ablaze in terror. The fiery barn walls collapsed and crashed inward, shooting up a volcano of sparks and glowing embers. Six black shadows fled the burning wreckage, their cries drowning in the night's fury. They escaped across the muddy road and through the adjacent field, finally settling down in the dark refuge of the nearby woods. The fur on their arched backs had been singed, their bony legs splattered with blots of mud. Here they'd lick their wounds till a new morning arrived.

The storm raged on for several more hours as the flames devoured the crumbling barn, leaving it a tangled mess of burning beams. Not until shortly before dawn did the lightning cease and the thunder die, and the rains diminished to a drizzle. The first dull light of morning painted a gray edge above the eastern horizon. The countryside was again a quiet place and the mice at last found a few moments of restful sleep. Lingering night fears slowly melted from their trembling limbs.

The remains of the barn lay as a smoking pile of sickly wet ash and charcoal-gray timbers. Its six previous inhabitants had crossed the road to find new dwellings.

Somewhere closer to the mice.

Where they'd be watching…

Waiting…

CHAPTER TWO

News From Across the Road

Morning arrived cool and wet as dewy blades of meadow grass sparkled in the hazy summer sun. Last night's storm swept away stale air that had been lingering over the countryside for days, replacing it with a crisp earthy fragrance. Sparrows, blackbirds and crows rocketed across the skies, while squadrons of dragonflies zipped curiously around a tangle of cattails towering beside a frog pond. Legions of grasshoppers bounded from one thicket of weeds to the next.

Several field mice scampered wildly about, sloshing through the wet grass or nibbling on patches of clover. Gabriel, a young mouse, stood on his large hind feet, grasping a dandelion with his pinkish claws and licking cold water droplets that dotted the stem. He was the size of a lemon with a tail almost twice as long. Chestnut brown fur sprouted near the tip of his nose right down to his hindquarters, with lighter patches of blond and white woven along the sides and underneath. Two charcoal-black eyes were fixed above Gabriel's nose like shiny round buttons, and a pair of semi-oval ears popped up near the tip of his head.

His friend Simon, a slightly smaller and sandy-colored mouse, nibbled on a wild mushroom nearby. Simon's scaly tail wiggled like a snake as he grasped a bit of the mushroom with his sharp claws. His white whiskers vibrated as he speedily chewed on the tasty morsel.

"What a terrific storm *that* was," Simon said between mouthfuls. "But it sure does wonders for these mushrooms. How they've grown!"

"Unfortunately the heavy rains weren't kind to all things. I heard that Fred and Doris were flooded out of their hole again," Gabriel said. "Third time this year!"

Simon bit off another tiny chunk from the mushroom. "That'll teach them for staying so close to the stream."

"Doris likes living by the water, so I suppose they'll find a new hole till the other dries out," Gabriel surmised. "By the way, have you seen Livingston today?" he inquired, scratching behind his ear. "I haven't had a glimpse of our silly friend since the sun was high in the sky yesterday."

Gabriel, Simon and Livingston were the best of friends who lived near each other in the field. They made their home in small holes dug beneath a clump of thorn bushes beside a grassy knoll. Many other mice lived scattered about in the field situated between a vast expanse of dark woods to the north and a lazy winding country road to the south. A narrow stream flowed out of the woods into the field, where it branched off in two directions.

One part of the stream flowed south towards the road, gurgling underneath an old wooden bridge before finally emptying into a nearby river. The other branch ran east, channeling into a frog pond covered with fleshy green lily pads and surrounded by an army of cattails. Several small trees shadowed the pond, providing the resident bullfrogs plenty of cooling shade on sweltering summer days.

Several other mice soon stopped by to chat with Gabriel and Simon during their morning forage. Not surprisingly, the conversation bubbled with remarks about last night's storm. Some had believed the community of mice would be flooded out of their homes, while others thought that a torrent of mud and water would bury them all before sunrise. Everyone, though, expressed joyous relief that the worst had passed.

"In all my days, I've never seen lightning dance so wildly in the clouds," old Thackery mouse said. He was a gray and black mouse with long white whiskers who greedily nibbled on a blade of grass with his sharp front teeth. "Why, the thunder echoed in my ears till this very morning!"

"And some trees on the other side of the stream nearly toppled over!" Florence added as she excitedly bounced on her hind legs. Her skinny reddish-brown body thinned out to an almost perfect point at the nose. "What a completely dreadful night!"

The chattering went on for several uninterrupted minutes as each mouse tried to top the other in his description of the storm. Monstrous! Awful! Frightful! Horrific! The images flew as thick as flies around a bushel of sweet corn.

"Has *anyone* seen Livingston?" Gabriel finally interrupted. "He hasn't been around since yesterday before the storm. What if he's lost—or worse? Maybe we should look for him."

Simon carelessly twirled his tail. "Livingston is the last mouse in the field you need to worry about. Trust me. Nothing fazes him. I'll bet he squeaked with delight last night when the storm let loose."

Simon's comment did little to comfort Gabriel, though he admitted that Livingston *did* have a tendency to run off on a whim, most often in search of an extra meal. "I just wish he'd behave more responsibly. He'll end up in a fix for sure one of these days. Mark my words."

There were murmurs of agreement among the other mice just as a blackbird fluttered upon the scene. He stretched his glossy wings after landing and bobbed his head back and forth when stepping about. A set of piercing yellow eyes, dotted black in the center, diligently scanned the ground for a moment. Splashes of purple appeared on top of his head when the sun reflected off him at just the right angle.

"Morning greetings to one and all!" he squawked.

"You're in extremely high spirits today, Orville," remarked Simon.

"And why not? The worms are especially plentiful. There's nothing like a rousing storm to bring the wigglies up to the surface," Orville said. "My family and I have already feasted."

"Did the storm do any damage to your nest?" Florence asked.

"Certainly not! I am a master weaver," Orville said indignantly. "Aside from some minor maintenance, which I have already attended to, my nest is as good as new."

"I'm happy to hear that," she replied while nosing for a quick snack.

"In the meantime, that has afforded me a chance to survey the damage across the road," Orville continued. "A rather cheerless sight, I'm afraid."

Simon's curiosity got the best of him, so he scampered over to Orville and stood on his hind legs, staring up at the blackbird's long narrow beak. "Survey the damage, did you say? What damage, Orville? What are you talking about?"

The bird flapped his wings again, causing the others to jump. "Don't any of you know what happened last night? Of course you can't fly, so I shouldn't be surprised at your usual ignorance of matters far and away from here."

"Oh, don't keep us wondering!" Simon persisted. "Tell us what you know." The other mice echoed Simon's plea, so Orville quickly gave in, disappointed that the mice weren't up for guessing games.

"Very well. I'll tell you," Orville said. "That abandoned barn across the road—that slouching old wreck of a dilapidated barn— burned to a cinder last night. Struck down flat by a bolt of lightning!"

Gabriel's interest was also piqued. "Are you telling the truth, Orville?"

"Of course! Why, I flew over the remains myself a short while ago. Nothing left but a pitiful pile of charred and smoking timbers. Awful stench."

The abandoned barn had been built over fifty years ago in a smaller field across the road not far from the river. A few of the more adventurous mice, on occasion, had viewed the structure when daring to wander near the road. None, however, had summoned up the courage to cross the road and examine the building up close. In fact, none of the mice in the field had *ever* crossed the road for any reason. Their side of the field provided more than enough food and space to keep them content for countless generations.

"Orville, did you see the actual lightning strike?" Gabriel inquired. "I thought I heard an especially loud crash close by last night, but figured it was just a noisy thunder clap."

6

"That barn being splintered into a million bits is what you heard!" Orville assured him. "Didn't any of you even see the orange and red glow of the roaring fire as it consumed the barn, plank by rotten plank?"

The mice avoided looking directly at Orville, being too embarrassed to tell him that they had been hiding deep inside their homes during much of the storm. The most anyone had seen was the pitch blackness of the underground earth.

"But now that you mention it, I think I *did* hear a loud crash," one of the mice said, trying to put on a brave face.

"Me too," another quickly added. "I'm—I'm sure of it!"

"Hmmm," Orville said, casting a skeptical glance before he snapped up a tiny slug crawling under him. "I suppose I shouldn't expect you fur balls to be out during a drenching storm, but haven't any of you *at least* noticed the smoke from across the road? That old barn is still puffing away and smelling up the other field next to the river."

The mice turned towards the south and gazed up at the sky. Orville was right. Off in the distance against a hazy blue background, wisps of dirty gray smoke drifted lazily into the air, intertwining like a brood of restless snakes. Gabriel climbed a small mound nearby for a better look. Here the grass was shorter and Gabriel stood on his hind feet, his nose pointed curiously in the air as his charcoal eyes scanned the somber skies. The eerie sight disturbed him so he quickly rejoined the others.

"There's nothing left but a pile of burnt timber," Orville continued. "I heard all sorts of caterwauling coming from that area last night after the lightning hit. Something must have been living in that barn, though I'm sure whatever it was isn't alive today."

Old Thackery mouse ambled to the front of the group. "I've heard similar noises from across the road late at night many-a-times. Strange things living in that barn, I suspect. Or *lived*."

"Beasts," Orville whispered. He held his wings aloft and glared at the mice, casting a groping shadow across them. "Prowling beasts with green eyes that glow in the dark. Stealthy creatures they are too, sneaking about so quiet... Quiet..." Orville lowered his head. "Then they pounce!" He snapped his beak at them, causing the mice to jump backwards and squeak. Orville squawked in delight, then folded his wings and snapped up another bug.

"Mind your manners!" Florence said, quivering slightly. "That wasn't funny, Orville. Why, I've heard stories about those beasts too. Dreadful stories. Mice from the other side of the road have passed through our parts on occasion and mentioned things. But I… I won't go into details!"

Gabriel wasn't easily intimidated by these rumors, but even he could recall hearing strange high-pitched noises coming from the south on certain nights. And the largest structure across the road in that direction was the very barn Orville had so vividly described.

"Even if these beasts do exist, they've never given *us* any trouble," Gabriel said. "There's a whole other field down that way near the river to keep them occupied. No reason for them to cross the road into ours."

"Maybe the lightning destroyed them," Simon added. "How could any creature escape such a terrible fire?"

"That's if they ever *existed* to begin with!" a voice scoffed in the distance.

Suddenly Livingston bounded into the crowd and squeaked with delight when noticing he had startled his companions. The chubby charcoal-gray mouse was famous for both his appetite and his less-than-serious nature.

"Just where have you been hiding, Livingston?" asked Gabriel. "No one has seen you since yesterday. I thought you might have gotten lost in the storm."

"Gabriel, you worry too much," he said, wiggling his nose. "I sneaked out early this morning to a secret blackberry bush I found close to the pond. The rain knocked many of the berries to the ground, so I had a tasty breakfast and took a nap before returning here," he explained. "There was no need to be concerned about me. It's *you* I'm concerned about, believing in those stories of beasts. What utter nonsense!"

Orville traipsed over to Livingston and flapped a wing right in front of his nose. "Insolent mouse! Stuffed with blackberries and thinks he knows better than I! Well, my furry friend, you can believe in the stories or not, but I'd trust my instincts if I were you. There's been something unsavory dwelling in that barn for as long as I can remember. The only question now," Orville softly said with a glint of a warning in his eyes, "is what's become of it?"

"Claptrap!" Livingston insisted. "I can understand Simon and some of the other mice believing in ridiculous tales, but I thought *you* had a sharper mind, Orville. Been flying under the hot sun too much lately?"

Orville snapped his beak at Livingston. "Believe as you wish, foolish one. But don't say you weren't warned, mouse!" With that, Orville stretched his wings and took to the skies, squawking a goodbye as he flew out of sight.

In spite of Livingston's arguments to the contrary, most of the other mice sided with Orville. They tended to believe in the existence of some type of beast inhabiting the barn before the storm hit, though none had actually seen the creature. And that suited the field mice just fine.

By noontime, the skies turned brilliant blue, the air warmed comfortably and all the talk of beasts and barns and lightning storms had faded. The mice played in their field and later foraged for blackberries after Livingston agreed to reveal his secret spot. No one even paid attention to the traces of smoke still lazily drifting up from the south.

Late that night, when the field lay still and silent except for the monotonous chirping of the crickets, Florence busily cleared some tiny pebbles and old weed roots from her living quarters. She felt restless and unable to sleep and hoped a bit of cleaning might tire her. When she heard a rustling noise in the grass outside her hole, she thought one of her friends was about to pay her an evening visit.

Florence abandoned the small pile of pebbles and roots she had gathered and scurried to the entrance of the hole. She poked her pointy nose into the darkness and felt a brush of cool air against her whiskers. A first quarter moon dipped low in the west. Florence detected a strange rumbling noise nearby, and for some uneasy reason felt she had better duck inside. A black shadow suddenly passed over the entrance, temporarily blocking the moon from her view. A rustling in the grass continued. The rumbling noise now sounded like a low steady growl. Then the shadow passed and all was still. The moon reappeared and the crickets chirped on.

Florence shivered with fright, retreating to the deepest recesses of the hole where she lay down and curled up into a ball. A nightmarish sleep finally overcame her as she shut her eyes to the dreadful night.

CHAPTER THREE

Warning Signs

One afternoon several days later, Gabriel, Simon and Livingston scampered off to play along the upper branch of the stream between the woods and the frog pond. The three mice splashed in the water's edge and chased each other among the rushes and cattails under a broiling sun, squeaking and chattering the entire time. Livingston, soon huffing and puffing, stopped to rest for a moment even though his companions urged him to continue with their game. He collapsed on a spot of warm grass, his wet fur pressed into unruly clumps against his charcoal-gray body.

"I can't move another step until I catch my breath," Livingston panted. "You two carry on without me. I feel the time is ripe for a nap. A *long* nap."

"The time is *always* ripe for a nap as far as you're concerned," Simon bluntly remarked. "You'd have more energy, Livingston, if you didn't eat twenty times a day. But rest if you need to. I think I'll wander along the stream and explore. How about it, Gabriel?"

"Thanks, but I'll stay here with Livingston," he said. "I'm feeling a bit sluggish myself in this heat. We'll catch up shortly."

11

"Suit yourself," Simon said with a flick of his tail.

He left Gabriel and Livingston nibbling on some grass while he ventured west along the stream towards the woods. The cold water gurgled eastward, splashing over mossy rocks before finally emptying into the frog pond a short distance away. Bundles of rushes and cattails slowly thinned out as Simon nosed onward. The stream's edge grew grassy and the curious mouse scrambled through the leafy blades, inching closer and closer to the dark woods. Soon the banks turned pebbly with patches of rich soil here and there. The sun grew less bright as its rays filtered through the tips of several overhanging branches.

Simon stopped. He sniffed the ground near a few scattered stones and among stray weeds popping up along the bank. His tail danced erratically in a thin breeze. Then Simon discovered something that grabbed his interest and wouldn't let go—an indentation in the soil. He examined it with growing interest. At first Simon thought that an oddly shaped stone had been removed, leaving a small hollow mark in the ground. Then he noticed the impression had a pattern to it, and after studying the splayed set of grooves from every angle, Simon realized that he was staring at an animal's claw print.

He gazed at the formation with deepening curiosity, circling it several times. At one point he even placed his tiny claw inside. Simon then carefully made an imprint of his front claw in the soil next to the other. His imprint, however, paled in size. Simon quickly scratched it out of the dirt and resumed his study of the other print.

He wondered what type of animal would leave such an impression. The power that creature must have! Simon lapsed into a wild daydream, imagining himself possessing such power and strength, roaming the wild without fear and commanding fierce loyalty from all others. He savored the vision, forgetting himself for a moment until Gabriel called out, snapping his senses back to reality. Simon was annoyed by the interruption but quickly shook it off. He dashed away to rejoin his friends, though disappointed that he had to leave so soon.

When the three returned home later in the day, a commotion brewed in their field. A dozen mice were huddled around Orville who was spouting off some news that distressed him and his captive audience. Gabriel nudged Simon and Livingston closer to the front of the crowd. Orville gently bobbed his purplish head as he related his woeful tale.

From what Gabriel could make out, a terrible accident had befallen a pair of blackbirds in another section of the field yesterday at twilight. A bird named Lily had been wounded in an attack while searching for food around the base of her nesting tree.

"She managed to flutter away with a broken wing to save herself," Orville sadly said. "But when she returned to the tree with her mate a short time later, their nest had been knocked off its limb and the unhatched eggs inside were smashed and strewn all over the ground. We were shocked and appalled by this horrible act. Lily was so distraught that she couldn't even tell us much about the creature who had done this." Orville paused a moment as he sorrowfully scratched at the ground. "She did say that she noticed several other creatures prowling nearby in the dusky shadows. Lily died during the night."

The mice shuddered when Orville finished his story. Some were bitter at the news while others feared that the life of every animal in the field was in peril.

"Those beasts are behind this!" old Thackery mouse bellowed, his gray and black body shaking with contempt. "Not all of them died in that lightning blast it now appears. Why, they must have sneaked across into *our* field after the barn collapsed and are preparing to hunt us down. We're doomed!"

"But if it is the beasts, where are they hiding in the daytime?" Doris asked. Her home had since dried out nicely and she and Fred were again living along the western branch of the stream.

"They probably live in the woods," a mouse named Chester suggested. "No doubt about it. Most likely waiting for nightfall to strike again." Many nodded in agreement.

"What'll we do?" his younger brother Elmer questioned in near hysterics.

"Is there anything we *can* do?" Doris hopelessly asked.

Livingston plowed his way to the front of the crowd and smirked. "You're all losing your wits, every last mouse standing here! That is if you had any to begin with. You talk dramatically of beasts and stalking creatures, but I haven't seen one yet, or heard their chilling screeches some of you are so fond of mentioning." Livingston stood on his hind legs and shook his chubby body as if pretending he was scared. "Oooooooohhh!" he wailed sarcastically. "The beasts are coming! The beasts are coming! I'm trembling down to my very bones!"

Orville took offense at Livingston's theatrics and looked him straight in the eyes. "Even after all that has happened to Lily and her unborn, you still don't believe in those awful beasts?"

"No! Nor should you," Livingston insisted. "Just imagine the crimp they would put in my search for a delightful late-night snack!"

"Shame on you for treating this tragic matter so lightly!" Florence squeaked. She looked at the others with growing concern, almost afraid to speak. "I wasn't going to mention this for fear of frightening anyone, but now I realize that I must."

"Florence, what's troubling you?" Gabriel gently inquired.

Florence clasped her tail to steady her quivering limbs and wiggled her pointy nose. "A few nights ago while I was cleaning, I happened to hear some rustling in the grass. So I peeked outside." She seemed afraid to go on until Gabriel offered her a reassuring smile. "That's when I heard this strange sound, almost like a growl. Nearly scared me to death, it did! I was about to go back inside when— something in the distance passed in front of the low moon and cast a shadow over my home. Something *big* and *unfriendly*. I scrambled to the back of my hole for dear life and never stepped out till daylight."

Livingston ripped a clover from the field and started chewing on it. "So what does that prove, Florence?"

"It proves that one of those beasts is prowling about, Livingston. And nearer than some of us care to admit," she said, glaring at him.

Livingston sighed in disgust. "I said it before and I'll say it again. Claptrap! These stories are utter nonsense. Wild speculation! And just because a bolt of lightning hits a nearby barn and shakes you all up a bit."

Gabriel felt that his friend spoke far too unreasonably in the face of the evidence. "Then how do you explain that Lily's eggs were destroyed?"

"A nest can fall out of a tree by a gust of wind."

"And what about Lily's wounds? They were caused by *something*, weren't they? Explain how," Gabriel challenged, though Livingston couldn't satisfactorily address that point and squirmed back into the crowd.

Simon kept quiet during the conversation, intrigued by the fear and anxiety that the beasts—if they existed—leveled on the other mice. These phantom creatures had suddenly turned the field into a terrifying place to live. Simon wanted desperately to tell everyone about the claw print he had discovered near the stream. But for some unexplainable reason, Simon decided to keep that knowledge a special secret for himself. He felt slightly more powerful than his friends for doing so—which he took pleasure in—yet a bit detached from them as well. Maybe he'd tell them about the claw print later in the day, Simon decided. Or perhaps tomorrow.

The discussion continued until the next forage, though Orville had flown off well before then, calling Livingston an intolerable rodent before he departed. Many of the mice were frustrated in their efforts to convince Livingston of the danger that might descend upon their homes at any moment, but in the end reluctantly let him believe as he wished.

"I only hope he comes to his senses before it's too late," Gabriel said to Simon as the crowd dispersed. "Our friend is concerned more about tomorrow's breakfast than anything else."

"Livingston has always behaved like that," Simon recalled. "Never much of a worrier. And quite a napper!"

"I'll keep an eye on him, I suppose. For his own good. But in any case, we should investigate this business about beasts if we're ever to feel at peace in our field again," Gabriel said. "This whole affair leaves me very disturbed. Very disturbed indeed."

CHAPTER FOUR

The Search Begins

Fears about the existence of green-eyed beasts persisted over the next two days. The field mice talked about nothing else until they almost convinced themselves that such horrible creatures indeed lived in the nearby woods. Something had to be done soon to confirm their suspicions, or else the mice knew the rest of their days in the field would be filled with unending dread and anxiety.

"We must search for those scoundrels at once!" old Thackery mouse proposed as he sat atop a stone shaded by a clump of tall dandelions. Several other mice gathered round, noses wiggling and tails bobbing, eagerly listening to each word. "A party of our youngest and strongest mice should comb the edges of the woods to determine once and for all if these beasts really exist."

"*Youngest* and *strongest*?" Simon said suspiciously. "Does this mean you won't be joining the search party?"

"I'm an old mouse!" Thackery snapped, combing back his whiskers. "I can't go sneaking about tree roots and shadows at my age. Besides, someone has to stay behind to, uh, um—protect the women and children!" Thackery eyed those he deemed were the most capable mice for the job. "So, any volunteers for this glorious mission?"

Gabriel squeaked to himself in amusement as Thackery talked his way out of joining the search party, though he knew nobody would have expected the old mouse to go. Gabriel, however, agreed that a group should be formed at once to quickly settle the matter.

"Thackery has the right idea. Some of us must journey to the woods and spy out the edges. I'm convinced that beasts are lurking there, though I have yet to see one."

Despite rumblings of disagreement with the plan and concerns about safety, one dozen mice finally committed to the endeavor, excluding Livingston.

"You expect *me* to traipse after imaginary beasts in the deep dark woods?" he uttered in disbelief. "Think again! I realize your intentions are honorable, but really, you're wasting your time. The lot of you have been so riled up into hysterics by questionable stories and half-truths that now you don't know *what* to believe. Yours is a foolhardy mission." Livingston plodded over into the shade of the dandelions. "I have absolutely no intention of frittering away this lovely day. There are more important things to do."

"Such as?" Gabriel inquired.

Livingston rapidly scratched behind an ear as he sat on his hind legs, and then jumped on all fours. "Such as searching for more blackberries!" he exclaimed before bounding off to find a late-morning snack.

Simon snapped his tail. "A big help *he* turned out to be. I hope a beast chases Livingston away from every blackberry bush he finds!"

"Don't talk like that, Simon, even in jest," Gabriel cautioned. "Livingston isn't always the most sensible mouse, but don't wish awful things on anybody. We can't let fear and anxiety cloud our senses."

However, as the search party prepared to embark on its journey to the woods that afternoon, uneasy thoughts about the creatures were *all* that the mice had in mind. Nothing else seemed to matter.

The early afternoon sun rose high in an ocean blue sky, baking the field below. A steady buzzing of insects competed with intermittent chirps, caws and squawks from several birds swooping through the air or alighting on nearby trees and shrubs. The twelve mice began their trek through tufts of warm grass without as much as a word exchanged among them. Their hearts felt heavy and their resolve uncertain. The prospect of entering the woods was something each mouse would gladly forfeit now that the journey had begun, but no one had the courage to say so to his friends.

Except for an occasional jaunt near the outlying trees, none of the mice living in Gabriel's section of the field had ever stepped into the woods. They had all the food, space and water they needed where they lived, so visiting the forest was not a high priority. Here the trees grew close together so that the sun barely managed to drop a ray of light inside. Bunches of leafy weeds sprouted along parts of the forest floor, and damp patches of moss lay upon rocks and dead tree branches like old blankets in a musty attic.

Before mid-afternoon, much sooner than expected, the mice inched close to the border of the woods. They gathered near a pile of pine cones that had fallen from a tree towering over them like a silent giant. After an uneasy few minutes arguing about how to begin, Gabriel suggested that the team split into pairs to cover more ground in less time.

"Let's return to the field before sundown and report our findings," he said. "And please, everyone, be careful!"

Each mouse wished every other one good luck, and then they broke up into teams of two and crawled inside the woods from different directions. With noses sniffing, eyes shifting and ears alert, all wondered if they'd ever see their warm fragrant field again.

Gabriel and Simon paired up and bravely entered, zipping past several trees over a layer of dry crumbling leaves. The air was cool and earthy smelling, and sounds from the nearby field seemed miles away.

They paused by a gnarly root at one point to study the surroundings. Simon pointed his head in every direction. "I didn't expect this place to look so inviting," Simon pleasantly remarked. "Less stuffy than I imagined. I suppose one could get used to living under trees."

"These woods may appear somewhat pleasing to the eye, Simon, but I sense something quite *unnatural* lurking inside," Gabriel whispered. "My stomach feels a bit queasy now, as if part of me doesn't want to go any farther. But I suppose we must for the sake of our friends back home."

So they marched boldly along under leafy and piny boughs until they were immersed in a sea of black shadows. Their eyes slowly adjusted to the dim light as they scrambled around a patch of damp vegetation growing near an especially large tree trunk.

"How can anyone even begin to call this a pleasant home?" Gabriel said. "Dark, stuffy and cluttered. Cool over there, warm over here. And menacing trees staring down at you constantly like hawks. I'll take a grassy field in the sunshine any day."

"I hope nobody living here takes offense at that unflattering description," Simon remarked while inspecting a tree root. "Remember, we're uninvited guests."

"I take your meaning. With any luck, maybe the owners won't be around today."

After exploring the immediate area and finding nothing of interest, the two mice summoned up the courage to delve deeper into the trees. Gabriel and Simon kept close to each other as they poked their noses into weed clumps and under tree roots, some that popped out of the ground and grew like wild roller coasters. Both even dared to scamper across a fallen tree to scan the surroundings for any sign of beasts or other unsavory forest creatures. But when an hour, then two, had drifted by without the faintest sign of another animal, Gabriel wondered if Livingston's theory might make sense after all.

"This is the most unadventurous adventure I've ever been on," he muttered. "Tree roots and *dry* leaves. Tree roots and *wet* leaves." Gabriel yawned. "I wonder how the others are faring."

Not wanting to jump to any rash conclusions, Simon suggested they snack on a piece of fungus he discovered, and then continue their expedition for a couple more hours. Only a thorough search would lend any credence to the idea that the creatures were nothing more than figments of their imaginations.

"Besides, here's a particularly succulent morsel I've rounded up," Simon said, pleased with himself. "We can't let it go to waste."

"Very well," Gabriel said as he nibbled on the food, which he admitted *was* very tasty.

Several minutes later, full and refreshed, Gabriel and Simon shot across the forest floor to choose another section to explore. A large mossy boulder caught Simon's eye, so he immediately dashed towards it and climbed to the top. The moss felt cool and soft as his claws sunk into it. A few times he rolled over and over, rubbing his back against the mossy blanket, flapping his tail and having a grand time. Gabriel, meanwhile, scurried up tree trunk after tree trunk, clutching slippery bark ridges with his sharp claws and studying the terrain a few feet below. Each found plenty to entertain himself during that woodland search.

Simon, squeaking contentedly, misjudged his speed at one point while attempting short leaps on top of the boulder. He sailed off the edge of the rock, grabbing just in time onto some moss growing over the edge and trying desperately to clamber up. Though the potential fall wasn't very far or dangerous, Simon was more worried about how much his pride might be injured should he lose his grip. But the moss proved too slippery and he couldn't hold on or climb back up. So Simon fell, landing deep into a pile of soft ferns.

Gabriel witnessed his friend's fall while descending a nearby tree trunk and raced over. "Simon! Are you all right?" he called out, racing around the soft green fronds, some laced with delicate spider webbing and dew drops.

"Yes, I am fine," he muttered with embarrassment, still hidden among the ferns.

Gabriel tried to suppress a laugh. "Then come on out so we can finish our search and go home. I'm growing weary of this place."

"Okay," Simon said, working his way through the clump of stems.

Gabriel waited, scratching at the ground, when he heard a rustle within the ferns. He looked up, prepared to see Simon poke through, when suddenly he heard his friend squeak in fright. Gabriel was about to burrow into the plants to help him when Simon darted out between two stems. He crashed head first into Gabriel and the two mice tumbled backwards. They quickly spun around when they heard something emerge from the ferns.

"Sssssssssssss! So I see I have some visitors today. How very lovely…sssss," hissed a leathery green and black speckled snake that weaved its way along the ground. "How very lovely indeed." It paused a short distance in front of the mice, gazing intently at them with its shifting blood-red eyes. "What brings you my way this afternoon?"

Gabriel and Simon stood frozen in fear, their small bodies quivering. "Pardon us for—for intruding," Gabriel stammered. "We're sorry if we disturbed you and will leave at—at once if you'd like."

"Leave without giving me a reason for this unexpected visit?" The snake sensed Gabriel's uneasiness and gently cast its forked tongue at him. The mouse yelped in terror. Simon, though, put his fear in check and seemed more fascinated than frightened by the taunting reptile. "I see that I've startled you," he said to Gabriel with enjoyment. "But your friend, ssssss, doesn't seem at all worried that I'll rush forward and gobble him up for an early supper."

Simon took a cautionary step back. "I'm not scared of you!" he piped up, though not quite sure why he had said that and amazed he had possessed the courage to do so.

"Sssssssssssss. Perhaps you *should* be scared!" The snake shot its lanky body into the air, looming above Gabriel and Simon as if ready to attack. But before the mice had a chance to think about fleeing, the snake coiled itself into its former resting place. "Ssssss, foolish rodents. Lucky for you I don't have an appetite now. But answer my question or I'll eat you both for sport. Why are you trespassing?"

Gabriel and Simon were in a muddle, so in order not to offend the snake and avoid becoming its next meal, they obeyed his wishes. Since Simon appeared reluctant to speak now, Gabriel took up the task.

"If you must know, my friend and I are searching through your interesting woods for beasts that have terrorized our field. We believe they may have taken refuge here recently, and want to make sure one way or the other. We're here for the sake of our families and friends only, and not to disturb you or cause any sort of trouble."

"Well your clumsy friend has already disturbed my nap, falling down on me from that rock!"

"Simon meant no harm," Gabriel said.

"Sssss… Perhaps not." The snake flicked its tongue several times as the rest of its body undulated in a shifting tangle. "So you think these beasts, sssss, might inhabit my woods, mouse?"

"Possibly." Gabriel inched a step closer to the snake, hoping to create a bond of trust. "Do you happen to know if any such creatures settled here since the last storm?"

The snake blinked its blood-red eyes a few times while slithering over and under itself, never once shutting its reluctant guests out of sight. It enjoyed having the mice unsure of its intentions and reveled even more in the fact that they were plagued by these so-called beasts.

"What difference does it make if these creatures live in my forest or not? Do you think they are the only beings that wish to cause you harm? For you see, sssss, even if the beasts didn't exist, there are always others ready to take their place. The inhabitants of these woods are many and crafty, and they, like me, are always watching. Always waiting."

"But we're not interested in any other creature," Gabriel politely informed the snake. "No one else from these woods has caused us any trouble that we know of. Only the beasts."

"Or maybe others *have* and you just don't realize it." The snake glided over a heap of rotting leaves, closing in on Gabriel who began to stare at the reptile as if lost in a paralyzing daydream. "Sssssssssssss. Many live in my shady woods, but it is up to you to sort out who are friends and who are foes."

Gabriel sensed that the snake was toying with him and would probably offer no help. He wondered how he and Simon could ever safely leave this place. Gabriel glanced at his friend for some unspoken advice, but Simon still gazed fixedly at the snake as if hypnotized.

"Well, thank you very much for your help," Gabriel managed to say. "But my friend and I must leave now and return home. Again, our sincerest apologies for disturbing your nap."

The snake flicked its tongue. "Sssss. What a shame you must depart so soon. I was hoping we might chat awhile longer, sssss, at least until my dinner time."

Gabriel shuddered. "Really, we must be on our way."

"Well, if you must, sssss, then you must," the snake soothingly agreed. "Far be it from me to keep you from your appointments. But do think of me should you ever pass this way again."

"We'll try," Gabriel answered stiffly.

"Just remember, sssss… I'm always here."

Before Gabriel could respond, the snake slipped out of sight in a flash. The forest stood deadly silent. Gabriel looked about suspiciously, wondering where the snake had disappeared to, when he thought he heard whispers near some distant trees. A host of black shadows wavered beneath the branches. Dots of green glowing light blinked on and off amid the shifting dark mass.

"Simon! We have to get out of here at once. We're in danger. I can feel it," Gabriel whispered, his voice strained and quavering.

But Simon stood as if half asleep, still staring at the place where the snake had lain. Gabriel had no time to deal with his friend's deepening bewilderment, so he dug his sharp claws into Simon's tail and yanked it, snapping him out of his stupor.

"Ow! What'd you do that for, Gabriel?"

"No time to explain, Simon. Just hurry and follow me! We have to leave *now*!"

Gabriel bounded off like a startled grasshopper and Simon reluctantly followed. At one point he thought he heard some whispers, so he stopped long enough for a quick look back.

"Who's there?" Simon cried out, straining his eyes in the gloom.

A flurry of shadows continued to weave in and out of the distant trees. Simon was convinced that he detected faint laughter. Then a disembodied voice called out to him. *"Remember, we're always here…"*

Simon didn't get a chance to respond for Gabriel scrambled back and urged his friend onward. The two raced through the woods at lightning speed, emerging from the trees as the sun began to dip in the west. They raced home without a backward glance.

CHAPTER FIVE

Finding A Friend

The sun dipped behind a feathery splash of red and purple clouds when Gabriel and Simon returned home. Others anxiously awaited their arrival, milling about like ants around a discarded piece of candy, eager to learn even the most trivial bit of news. Of the dozen mice that joined the expedition, four had already made it back, though with nothing of interest to report. Only when Gabriel and Simon rushed headlong into the crowd did the excitement reach its peak.

"What'd you find out?" Florence asked, though a part of her didn't want to know the answer. Her nose twitched in anticipation.

"The beasts are for real!" Gabriel blurted out, short of breath and heart pounding. "We didn't see them up close, but there's definitely something loathsome living in those woods. Simon and I barely escaped."

"Is that true, Simon?" Doris asked, standing next to her mate. Her dark fearful eyes were set in a tiny body the color of summer wheat. "I had hoped nothing would come of the search." Fred nuzzled close to Doris, trying to comfort her.

Simon distractedly dug his claws into the ground. "I guess there *are* things living in the woods," he answered hesitantly. "But we never actually saw any beasts face to face." He eyed his companions uneasily, trying not to look directly at Gabriel. "Still, I suppose Gabriel is correct," he admitted.

Gabriel squeaked at Simon's lack of concern and wondered why his friend was acting this way. He suspected Simon was putting on a brave face to impress the others.

"Please believe me. There *are* creatures living in the woods. We both saw them. How many, I cannot say, but they closed in on Simon and me as we left. Though I'm not sure why they didn't chase after us," Gabriel said with an air of suspicion. "They had plenty of opportunity."

"Awful news indeed!" old Thackery mouse said, shaking his head. "That last storm rained ill tidings upon us, and now we'll have to deal with them."

"But how?" others wondered aloud.

As the sun sank below the horizon, two more of the mice sent on the search finally returned. And though none of them had any sightings of beasts to report, they did discover a few large claw prints in the dirt at one spot near the edge of the woods.

"They looked freshly made," one said.

"Then that confirms Gabriel's story," Florence whispered while clutching her tail. "I don't think I like this."

Twilight deepened and a few white stars blinked on in the deep blue heavens. A gentle breeze sighed over the cool grass. Birds nesting in nearby trees grew eerily silent. Gabriel sniffed the air but found no comfort in his surroundings.

"Darkness will fall soon. I have a terrible feeling that the beasts may prowl in our section of the field tonight."

"How do you know for sure?" Fred asked, still calming Doris who was as jittery as a mosquito over water.

"I don't know how I know it. I just *do*!" Gabriel insisted. "We should all return to our holes immediately. It's not safe being out in the open right now. There'll be time enough tomorrow to continue our discussion."

"What about the others still searching?" old Thackery questioned. "I feel responsible for them. What if they're lost? It was my idea to track down those beasts. If anything happens to them..."

Gabriel scurried over to his friend. "Don't worry, Thackery," he said in a comforting voice. "They're resourceful mice. They'll make it back."

"Maybe one of us should run out and check on them to make sure they're not in trouble," Fred suggested.

"Perhaps you're right," Gabriel said.

Chester and his brother Elmer volunteered to search for the others and warn them that the beasts might be on the prowl. They raced out of sight, heading in the direction the mice originally went. The rest of the crowd broke up to return to the security of their homes. Florence offered to let Fred and Doris stay with her rather than risk going back to their hole by the stream. Doris, who was too anxious to travel even a short distance with danger lurking in the shadows, quickly snapped up the invitation.

When Gabriel and Simon returned to their burrows under a patch of thorn bushes along a grassy knoll, they were surprised to find that Livingston was nowhere in sight. They searched the immediate area, but found no sign of their capricious friend.

"Now where in this field could that senseless mouse have run off to?" Gabriel asked in disgust. "Can't he think about anything other than a late-night snack?"

"I'm sure he'll return before it's too dark," Simon said without much concern. "Livingston can take care of himself."

Gabriel sighed in the deepening shadows. "Under ordinary circumstances, maybe. But Livingston doesn't know that the beasts are on the prowl tonight."

"We don't know that for sure either," Simon said.

"*I* know it, Simon. I feel it in my bones. Those creatures saw us in the woods. They know that *we* know of their existence. They're surely going to attack sooner or later," he said. "Though I fear sooner. Livingston may be in grave danger. I'm going after him!"

Simon protested. "How will you know where to start looking, Gabriel? If the beasts plan to attack, then you're putting yourself in danger too."

"Doesn't matter. Livingston is my friend and I have to find him. I'll search around that blackberry bush he discovered near the stream the other day. Chances are that foolish mouse will be near food. Goodbye, Simon."

"You're the one who's being foolish!"

Gabriel ignored him and bounded off into the twilight shadows as the fiery summer stars burned as brightly as polished diamonds. Simon watched his friend disappear among the tall grass, and then scolded himself for being so callous.

"Oooooh, wait for me!" he muttered, racing off to catch up with Gabriel. "I'm going with you. We'll find that miserable Livingston together—no matter how much trouble he causes us!"

By the time they reached the upper branch of the stream, darkness had fully settled in. A nearly full moon rising in the east cast a pale silvery glow across the field. Gurgling stream water sparkled in the lunar light as it swished by, bobbing an army of cattails and wild grass that grew on its edges. Thousands of cricket chirps filled the air in a never-ending tune, while a chorus of bullfrogs croaked contentedly in the nearby pond.

Gabriel led the way towards the stream as Simon followed, then turned in the direction of the frog pond. Livingston's blackberry bush grew on the banks several yards before the stream emptied into the pond. Whether Livingston would be there was another matter. Gabriel wasn't sure if his search would be successful, but he went through the motions because he didn't know what else to do. Fear and frustration tormented him as they waded through the grass.

"The frogs are really raising a racket tonight," Gabriel whispered. "Do you think they suspect something out of the ordinary, Simon?"

"Hard to say. I think the crickets are louder than the frogs could ever hope to be. Anyway, Gabriel, I don't believe the frogs worry one whit about the beasts. No matter how deadly they are, I can't imagine them brave enough to jump into a slimy pond to catch an old bullfrog."

Gabriel prepared to echo his agreement when he caught a glimpse of the blackberry bush just ahead in the moonlight. "There it is, Simon."

"No doubt stripped of every morsel of fruit, if I know Livingston."

"We'll soon find out. Let's make a run for it."

The two mice rushed towards the blackberry bush, hoping to find their friend snacking away on the tasty bits of fruit, or possibly fast asleep underneath the tangle of branches. But when they arrived, there was no sign of Livingston.

"Maybe he went home already," Simon speculated.

"I hope so." Gabriel nosed about and found several half-eaten blackberries on the ground glistening in the moonlight. "Someone was here earlier, so perhaps it *was* Livingston. Though it's not in his nature to leave bits of a meal uneaten."

Simon picked up one of the plump berries and nibbled on it. "Still tasty. Very fresh, as if it was only picked a short time ago."

"Oh, where is that bothersome mouse!" Gabriel muttered, ready to call out to him.

Suddenly he froze. Gabriel heard a swishing sound in the tall grass off to their right. His ears perked up, listening, waiting. His eyes anxiously scanned the area. Gabriel urged Simon not to utter a sound as they quietly took refuge deep inside the blackberry bush.

Then they heard the noise again, closer this time, and louder, as if a sharp wind scraped across a pile of dry autumn leaves. Gabriel and Simon quivered, creeping backwards farther beneath the branches. Though quite hidden, they still could see the immediate area outside through small openings between the thin branches.

The noise increased. Something was creeping through the field only a few yards away. Soon a steady rumbling sound was audible, like the low growl of a stalking animal. Then Gabriel and Simon saw it straight ahead—a large, four-legged black figure heading directly towards them. There was no doubt in their minds. The beasts were real.

The two mice trembled as the creature closed in, its long bony legs swishing through the grass. Gabriel and Simon looked at each other, preparing to run out through the back of the blackberry bush, when the beast suddenly changed direction and wandered towards the forest. It hadn't spotted them.

As the beast passed by, Gabriel saw its ghastly green eyes glowing in the moonlight. Its ragged furry face was scratched every which way, with two torn and pointed ears fixed on top. A set of sharp fang-like teeth dripped with blood and saliva, and Gabriel flinched in horror at what he saw next. Clutched within the jaws of the beast, lifeless and limp, was Livingston. His tail swayed like a pendulum with every step the creature took as it slowly marched away. Gabriel and Simon shuddered. They never saw their friend again.

Several minutes drifted by before either mouse had the courage to come out from hiding. The shock of seeing Livingston dead had nearly driven all hope and spirit out of them. Neither said a word nor could imagine how to break the sad and terrible news to the others back home.

Then the swishing noises in the grass started again. Gabriel and Simon didn't hear it at first for they were lost in sorrowful thoughts. When they finally did, the mice instantly realized the horrible truth. The beasts were returning!

There wasn't a moment to lose. Grieving over Livingston's death would have to wait if they were to save themselves. Gabriel and Simon, eyeing each other but not uttering a sound, shot through the back of the blackberry bush like bullets, heading as close to the stream as they dared. They couldn't risk going back into the field yet, for the beasts were undoubtedly stalking everywhere. So the two followed the stream towards the frog pond, knowing this was the wisest course of action to protect themselves. Gabriel hoped they would have better luck surviving the night than Livingston.

CHAPTER SIX

A Possible Solution

Frogs and crickets. Their incessant croaking and chirping saturated the air like a blanket of stifling humidity on a hot summer night.

"I think we gave them the slip," Gabriel whispered.

An army of black cattails assembled on the stream's edge, gently bobbing as cool water flowed through their ranks.

"Are you absolutely sure?" Simon anxiously asked. "Without-a-doubt *sure*? As-sure-as-the-sun-rises *sure*?"

The moon continued a slow climb from the east, swishing through a field of stars as it gently dropped its light across the surface of the pond.

"Trust me," Gabriel assured his friend as he nosed about a bundle of grass. "The weeds around here are quite thick and kept us well hidden. If the beasts couldn't find us under the blackberry bush earlier, they'll never find us here. So crawl on out from your hiding spot."

"All right." Simon peered beyond his leafy cover, sniffed the air and deemed it safe enough to venture forth. "Do you think they're prowling around our field right now, Gabriel?"

"Most likely, though it pains me to say so."

"I don't feel right staying here, safe from all the trouble. Maybe we should have tried to run home instead."

Gabriel walked along the stream, signaling for Simon to follow. They were careful not to get too close to the edge. Countless cattails flourished in the area, and an array of flowering bushes and plants grew wildly, darkening the mice's path with coal-black shadows.

"We wouldn't have had a chance to make it safely back home, Simon. The beasts would have hunted us down in seconds. They're ruthless and deviously clever creatures." Gabriel hung his head low in grief. "Poor Livingston! If only we had reached the blackberry bush sooner. We might have warned him in time. We could have saved him."

Simon emitted a tiny squeak in agreement, and then neither said anything more for a while. Though their efforts had proved fruitless, Gabriel and Simon knew they weren't to blame for Livingston's death. They had tried their best, but nothing could bring him back. It was time to move on and find a safe spot to rest until sunrise. Only then could they risk a trip back home and find out how the others had fared this awful night. Only then could they deliver the sorrowful news about Livingston. Yet in the back of their minds, Gabriel and Simon wondered if their friends at home would still be alive by the time the sun peeked over the eastern hills.

The pair eventually reached the point where the gurgling stream converged with the lazy stillness of the frog pond. The water lay covered in lily pads, surrounded by a dense wall of cattails and overshadowed by several sprawling oak trees. Gabriel and Simon skirted the pond's edge for several yards, searching for a spot to spend the night. Despite the croaking clamor from hundreds of unseen frogs, the mice knew they would have no trouble falling asleep after their ordeal. They stopped to rest for a moment, and then realizing how tired they were, decided that this was the perfect spot to spend the night after all.

"I can't move another step," Gabriel said. "Not if all the beasts in the field were chasing me."

"I'm *nearly* that tired," Simon said. "But I do have a bit of strength left to crawl to the edge of the pond for a drink. I'm very thirsty." He trotted away, relieved to wander about without having to watch for signs of the enemy.

"Don't stray too far, Simon. I don't want to have to look for you in the middle of the night. I've had enough excitement for one day."

"Don't worry, Gabriel. I can take care of myself," he said while about to take a drink from the pond.

But as he brought his head close to the water, the ground beneath his feet seemed to waver and get wet. Instantly he tumbled head first into the pond, sinking like a stone. The water wrapped around his body like the grip of cold deadly fingers. He finally rose to the surface, paddling his hind legs as fast as he could.

Gabriel turned when he heard the noise. "Simon?"

"Help me, Gabriel!" he squeaked, thrashing about in the chilly water. "Hurry!"

Unfortunately, because of the darkness, Simon didn't realize that he had stepped beyond the border of the pond and walked across several lily pads growing near the shore. As he leaned over to drink, he stood right on the edge of one lily pad that quickly gave way, sending him under for a late night bath.

"Simon!"

Gabriel raced to his friend's aid, but didn't know how to save him. He watched helplessly as Simon splashed in the water, desperately trying to grab onto the slippery edges of the lily pads without success. Since Gabriel couldn't swim either, he didn't dare jump in to attempt a rescue. But he knew he had to do something before it was too late. Gabriel had already lost Livingston to the beasts. He couldn't bear the thought of losing another friend.

"I—I can't hold out… much longer…" Simon struggled, nearly out of breath.

"Grab onto the lily pad, Simon! Sink your claws into the leaf!"

"I'm… trying…"

Every time Simon slapped his claws against the fleshy leaf, they would slide down, unable to rip through the leaf to secure a hold. Simon grew tired. His strength quickly drained from his limbs. His hind legs felt like heavy stones from constantly treading water. He had only moments left.

Gabriel, nearly in a panic, decided to venture out onto the lily pad. Simon was his friend and it was his duty to try to save him despite the danger. Perhaps Simon could latch onto his tail and he could pull him to safety—or else be dragged into the water himself where they would both drown. None of their friends would ever know what happened to them.

Gabriel gingerly stepped onto the first lily pad near the shore and crawled slowly along its bobbing surface. Simon still splashed in the water, tearing at the air and lily pads in a hopeless bid for freedom. Gabriel didn't have much time to act, so he moved faster along the slippery surface, carefully watching where one edge of a lily pad ended and another began so he wouldn't fall through like Simon.

"I'm almost there, Simon. I'll save you. Hang on for another moment!"

"I... can't... Gab..."

Simon splashed some more as he attempted to scurry up the lily pad, but his strength was all but sapped. Gabriel was now only inches away. Simon made one last-ditch effort to dig his claws into the leaf—but they wouldn't catch. Gabriel started to lunge after him, but it was too late. Simon sank below the surface, exhausted, his arms sliding helplessly down the edge of the lily pad. Gabriel caught a pale gleam of moonlight in his friend's eyes as the pond water engulfed him.

Gabriel squeaked in horror, spinning in circles on the lily pad, wanting to jump in the pond after Simon, though knowing it would mean his own death. He couldn't lose two friends in one day. But before Gabriel performed such a courageous yet foolish act, something out of the ordinary occurred.

Suddenly, as if by a strange magic, Simon rose slowly out of the water. The sandy-colored mouse, sitting on his hind legs, appeared to float above the lily pad. Water droplets, beaded along his white whiskers like a string of Christmas lights, burned with reflected moonlight. Simon coughed and sneezed several times in his bedraggled state. Gabriel looked up at his weightless friend, unable to believe his eyes. Simon was too soaked and confused to realize what was happening. His fur stuck to his sides like wet carpeting.

33

"Simon!" Gabriel whispered in amazement, still staring up at his dazed friend. "How can this be happening to you? How?"

"It's not a terribly difficult puzzle to solve if you would only look this way," a deep voice said with a tinge of irritation.

Gabriel cast his eyes down, and to his surprise, saw a yellowish pair of eyes staring back at him just below Simon's feet. Simon, also startled by the strange voice, looked below and found himself perched atop the head of an enormous green bullfrog.

"Er, hello," Simon muttered, still dripping.

"Hello, yourself," the frog said, rolling his eyes. "Now if it wouldn't be too much trouble, please kindly remove your furry wet self from my body. Though this may come as a shock to you field dwellers, we frogs generally *don't* enjoy lugging rodents around on our heads."

"Of course not," Gabriel said in amusement.

"I'd be happy to step off," Simon said to the patient frog, staring at him upside down and eye to eye. "If you'd only paddle back to shore, I'll be ever so grateful. Just get me away from these dreadful lily pads."

"Oh, it will be my life's *ultimate* pleasure," the frog muttered sarcastically as he waded to shore.

Simon quickly scooted off the amphibian and hugged the ground as if he'd never let go. He shook the remaining pond water out of his fur as Gabriel rejoined him on shore. The two raced in circles, tails waving, happy to be alive. Then Simon turned to his rescuer, still lounging in the water, and thanked him properly.

"I am in your debt, frog. I wouldn't have survived another moment if you hadn't come along."

"Probably not," the frog remarked indifferently. He appeared still as stone while soaking in the pond, nearly blending in with the water this time of night.

"I'd like to thank you for saving my friend, too," Gabriel added.

"Yes, yes, yes," the frog said. "I accept your thanks from one and all. If only tasty flies were as abundant as your gratitude. Oh, well..." He blinked his large eyes a few times as he studied the two mice. "Now that you've learned you're not very good swimmers, please tell me exactly who you *are*? And why are you hanging around my pond raising all sorts of racket?"

"I'm Gabriel, and my friend you lifted out of the water, is Simon."

"Names are a start. But where are you from and why are you here?" he inquired. "Are there others around like you who plan to prowl about my pond in the darkness, or perhaps try to drown in it?"

"Just the two of us," Simon answered. "We had only planned to stay till sunrise, if that's not a problem. You see, we were running from danger and felt this pond would provide us refuge during the night."

The frog scanned the mice with his slippery bulging eyes, certain they were harmless, yet curious about the source of the danger Simon mentioned. "Precisely what were you running *from*? I'd like to know."

Gabriel picked up the story at this point. "A few nights ago during that terrible storm, a barn across the road from our field was destroyed by lightning. Though we had never seen them, we have heard rumors that several green-eyed creatures lived inside that barn. Unfortunately for us, they crossed the road and are now hiding in the woods close to our home. Simon and I had a run-in with them a short time ago. Since we couldn't risk going back to our field till daylight, we came here instead where it's safer."

The frog believed Gabriel's story and gave a thundering croak as a sign of approval. "So you've been troubled by these so-called beasts, have you? Pesky things, no doubt. My friends and I are annoyed by others on occasion as well."

"The beasts come to this pond?" Gabriel piped up. "Then we're not safe even now!"

"Calm down," the frog said. "I'm not referring to the animal beasts plaguing you. I was talking about the two-legged type. They wander out here casting their lines with shiny hooks and bother our fish friends. We frogs have to watch out for those sharp pointy devices too."

"I see," Simon said, trying to sound sympathetic, but finding the frog's occasional inconvenience hardly comparable to the constant terror of the beasts.

The frog submerged himself for a moment to cool down, and then drifted back closer to shore. "I believe your story, my young mice, but I have a feeling that you left something out. I detect a trace of melancholy in your voices, as if another matter troubles you. Am I correct?"

"You are," Gabriel said, his voice cracking. He then told the frog about the sad fate of Livingston near the blackberry bush. "Our friend often wandered off looking for an extra meal."

"Or a quick nap," added Simon.

"I wouldn't be surprised if Livingston visited your pond now and then," Gabriel continued, fondly recalling his friend. "He *did* enjoy his life though."

"If he visited my pond, I never saw him," the frog replied, deeply moved by Gabriel's account. "But however much you miss your friend, it is you two who need to be protected now. I have decided to let you spend the night beside the pond. You may stay as long as you wish."

"Thank you. Though just until sunrise will be sufficient," Simon assured him. "We need to get home as soon as possible."

Gabriel nibbled carelessly on a grass blade, thinking about the problems that still faced them. "I hope everyone at home survives the night. Simon and I gave our friends plenty of warning about the beasts," he said, looking distressfully at the frog, the blade of grass locked between his teeth. "But I fear we'll never have a peaceful life again. None of the animals in our field, except possibly the birds, can escape the fury of the beasts."

The frog thought for a moment, ducked underwater, then suddenly leaped up and landed on one of the lily pads with a terrific splash. He rose and fell upon the undulating leaf for a few seconds as water rolled off his back, then signaled for Gabriel and Simon to approach. The two mice inched close to the edge of the pond.

"I can't help seeing the gloom and frustration haunting you both. That raging storm has cast mayhem and madness upon your community," the frog began. "My fellow frogs and I were quite pleased when the rains fell. The pond water rose and the cattails and flowers grew and blossomed at an astounding rate. We delighted in the deluge." He croaked again, his chest expanding like a balloon. "You mice, however, were not so lucky. A misdirected lightning bolt and—BOOM! Your way of life was rocked off its foundation. Luckily for you, I know what you can do to survive."

"You do?" Gabriel asked, his eyes wide with anticipation. "You know how to get rid of the beasts?"

The bullfrog snapped his tongue at a passing moth and reeled in a snack. "Listen, I'm not a miracle worker," he said, swallowing his meal with relish. "I can't get rid of the beasts anymore than you can."

"Then what's your great plan?"

"Simply this—find a new home."

"What?"

"You heard me, Gabriel. And if you look deep in your heart, you know it's the only way. No matter how many mice live in the field, your numbers are no match for those beasts." The frog's statement bristled with cold logic. "From what you've told me, those creatures will be on the prowl night after night, making you prisoners in your homes. What if one day they get the courage to hunt you down in the sunshine? Then your days are surely numbered, my friends. It's only a matter of time."

Gabriel and Simon found no comfort in the frog's blunt words, yet reluctantly admitted that he spoke the truth. How could a band of small mice, outmatched in both strength and speed, compete with the deadly force of the forest creatures? It was impossible. Their only hope for survival lay in fleeing the field in secret and searching for a new home.

"Though I hate to agree with you, frog, I must," Gabriel said. "Maybe a new home *is* our only chance, but I'm not certain that the other mice would agree. We love where we live now, and many of the older mice couldn't bear to leave no matter what the consequences."

"Then it is *your* job to convince them otherwise, at least those young and brave enough to make a new start. If you really wish to escape the wrath of the beasts, then I see no other way." The frog lapped up a beetle scuttling across the dirt and swallowed it.

"I suppose you're right," Gabriel said, looking at Simon for support. But Simon merely wiggled his nose in uncertainty.

"Then again, this is a frog giving a mouse advice. I'm not in the danger you are and don't have to hop away to new living quarters. So think hard about what you must do." The bullfrog jumped back in the water with another colossal splash, nearly soaking Gabriel and Simon to the skin. "A final word before I leave. No one can make this important decision for you, because only *you* know if you possess the will and the courage to move on. But *if* your decision is yes," he said, his eyes blinking out the moonlight, "then I may be able to help you. There is, possibly, a solution to your troubles."

"Tell us!" Gabriel pleaded. "Where can we go to save ourselves?"

"Patience, my friend. I will not reveal my answer yet. But should you and others truly wish to find a new home, then return to this spot on the night after tomorrow. Bring whoever wishes to undertake a possibly treacherous journey. That is all I will tell you now."

Quickly, the frog dived deep into the pond and vanished, and soon the surface of the pond lay as smooth and reflective as a mirror. Gabriel and Simon, now alone and dejected, discussed the possibility of searching across the wild for another home. In spite of the threat from the beasts, they felt uncomfortable at the prospect of abandoning their field, the only home they had even known. Yet not to do so would spell their doom.

In the end, Gabriel and Simon agreed to deliver the bullfrog's proposal to their friends and return to the pond to hear him out. Then, unable to keep their eyes open a moment longer, the two drifted off to sleep as the crickets chirped and the frogs croaked deeply in the darkness.

They arose at the crack of a cool, gray and quiet dawn. The frog was nowhere in sight along the weedy edges of the pond. Gabriel wanted to have a final word with him, hoping to glean a few more clues about this mysterious new home. But the bullfrog never returned. So, eager to get back to the field, he and Simon dashed off. Answers to all their questions would have to wait.

CHAPTER SEVEN

The Debate

Gabriel and Simon returned home as the sun blazed above the eastern horizon like a yellow grapefruit balanced on a counter's edge. The other mice cheered upon seeing them, but when Livingston wasn't anywhere in sight, their emotions nose-dived into depths of shock and anguish. The news of Livingston's passing devastated the field mice. Though many admitted their friend had been carefree and too much of a dreamer, most held a deep fondness for Livingston and missed him terribly. Others wondered if they might suffer a similar fate.

The mice reminisced about Livingston throughout the early hours, mourning him in their own way. Fortunately, there had been no additional casualties during last night's raid by the beasts. The other mice were well protected in their holes. Chester and Elmer had successfully warned those returning late from the forest search party about the impending attack, bringing them safely back home too.

Not until the sun climbed high in the sky, and the mice had filled themselves during their noon forage, did Gabriel mention his and Simon's encounter with the bullfrog at the pond. He didn't want to blurt out the idea of searching for a new home, possibly scaring some away from the proposal at the start, so Gabriel eased his way into the topic. He insisted that Simon first tell of his harrowing adventure in the pond.

"Our friend nearly drowned himself," Gabriel chuckled. "Plop! Off the lily pad and into the cold water. I laugh now, but it wasn't funny at the time," he said, having everyone's rapt attention. He nodded to Simon as the other mice chattered among themselves in astonishment.

"Luckily our bullfrog friend raised me out of the water when he did, or I might have ended up as dinner for some of the local fish," Simon added on cue from Gabriel. The mice laughed, especially old Thackery mouse, though Simon wasn't amused in the least. But he played along as Gabriel wanted.

Simon quickly finished his story, touching only on the high points, and then let Gabriel fill in the colorful details, including the frog's offer of help in finding a new home. Many were taken aback at such a suggestion, despite Gabriel's casual attitude.

"Leave this field?" someone shouted. "That's ludicrous! Nonsense talk from someone who has been sitting under the hot sun for too long."

"I want to hear him out," another said. "Those beasts aren't leaving anytime soon. Maybe we *should* find a new place to live."

And so the debate began. The gathering of mice was a bobbing field of fur and tails, squeaking and jabbering and nosing about. Simon didn't feel much like talking anymore that afternoon, so when Gabriel gained control of the discussion under the sweltering sun, Simon stealthily nudged his way towards the back of the crowd and slipped out of sight through a bed of clover. Gabriel noticed his friend leaving, heading south, but said nothing, though something troubled him deep inside.

"Now quiet, everyone! Quiet! Let me speak uninterrupted for a moment please," old Thackery mouse said, squeezing to the front.

"Go ahead," Gabriel said. "I want to hear everybody's opinion."

"Then we might as well start with the most important one—mine!" Old Thackery brushed his whiskers and wiggled his nose, full of suspicion. "Now what is so special about this bullfrog fellow that he thinks he can help us find a new home? Think about it. A *bullfrog*?

I guarantee that wet and slimy green thing hasn't spent a single day of his life away from the pond. What in the wide field could such a croakster know about finding a home for mice? Answer me that—*anyone?*"

"I'm not sure I can," Gabriel replied. "The frog didn't provide us with any details, but I think we ought to give him a chance, Thackery. After all, he saved Simon's life and allowed us to spend the night in safety at the pond. I trust him. He looked like an honest frog."

"I don't *distrust* him," Florence added, clasping her tail with her nose pointed up. "But I'd sure like to know a lot more about his offer before we agree to anything." That seemed to be the general opinion as several took turns expressing their hopes and fears.

"So that's why we should go tomorrow night and meet with the frog," Gabriel insisted. "We're not committing to any course of action at this point. Let's just hear the frog out, learn what his plan is, *then* we can decide." A few mumbled their approval, more at ease since a final decision wasn't being made here and now, but still not enough were convinced. Gabriel then nonchalantly scratched behind an ear. "We can always return home if we don't like what we hear. Just don't expect to roam about the sweet cool grass at night ever again. And won't *that* be a treat when fresh mushrooms sit glistening in the moonlight, ripe for the picking. Oh, well..." He sighed gloomily. "I only hope those beasts never get daring enough and start prowling about during the day."

Such a possibility prompted another round of boisterous discussion, with a few mice insisting that the survival of the community depended upon leaving at once. Others still believed that the beasts would eventually move away, or deeply hoped so. All in all, it was a noisy meeting of mice that lasted well into the afternoon.

Finally, after tiring of the endless bickering, Chester stepped forward and asked for everyone's attention. "I've had more than enough time to think about it, and I say we take the chance and go. What harm can there be in just listening to what this frog has to say? We owe it to ourselves to find out what possibilities exist outside this field. We owe it to Livingston."

"That's the right attitude!" Gabriel said, greatly encouraged.

Then Florence marched up to the front of the crowd speaking in favor of the idea, followed by Elmer and several others too. One by one they voiced their approval till a total of forty-nine mice decided to venture to the frog pond in two night's time. Gabriel assumed Simon would go too, so that raised the number of travelers to an even fifty.

Gabriel was unanimously chosen to lead the group composed mostly of the younger mice. Many of the older couples were simply too attached to their homes in this part of the field to abandon them now, while others weren't physically prepared to handle such a long and dangerous journey should it come to that.

"I'll take my chances here," old Thackery boldly stated. "I've lived in this field all my life. I'm not about to let a few cranky beasts run me out of my home!" He rubbed his nose then spoke softly. "But I do wish you all the best of luck. Maybe if I were younger I might have gone. We'll miss you, but we understand why you must leave."

"Thank you," Gabriel replied. "We'll need all the good luck we can muster."

Later that day as the mice made hasty preparations for the next night's departure, Gabriel looked for Simon, but found no sign of his friend at home or at any of his favorite feeding spots. He scurried to the top of a small mound and scanned the horizon. The late afternoon sun cast lazy shadows that wiggled across the swaying grass. Sapphire blue skies offered a crisp backdrop for dozens of blackbirds streaking through the air. And though not a wisp of smoke rose in the south, Gabriel still cast an especially keen eye in that direction. He had an uneasy feeling in the pit of his stomach about the barn lying across the road in a pile of charred and brittle pieces.

Another hour or so passed before Simon finally returned to his hole underneath the thorn bushes. He was surprised to find Gabriel waiting for him inside.

"So here you are at last, Simon," he said, startling his friend. "I thought I might not see you again till tomorrow."

"What are you doing here, Gabriel?"

"Waiting for you, of course. Don't tell me you've taken after Livingston, running off on the spur of the moment." Gabriel waited patiently for a reply.

Simon stood on his hind legs, reluctant to speak. "Not exactly. I just felt like being alone for a while. I'm sorry I left the meeting early."

Gabriel squeaked with delight. "You'll be happy to know that forty-nine of us have decided to go to the pond tomorrow night to find out what the bullfrog has to say. Fifty if you come along."

"That's good news," Simon remarked without much enthusiasm.

"So will you join us?"

"Why—of course. Well—why wouldn't I?" he asked, almost rudely.

"Good. I'm glad." Gabriel headed for the opening and sniffed the summertime air. "Let's go get some dinner, Simon, and you can tell me all about your afternoon. Where you went and the like."

"I don't think—"

"Now no excuses!" Gabriel insisted as he bounded out of the hole. "Hurry. I'm famished."

Simon reluctantly followed.

The pair found a patch of tall dandelions growing alongside a small rotting tree limb crawling with a variety of bugs, slugs and caterpillars. They feasted like kings! Not until they were stuffed and resting in a tuft of grass did either speak a word.

"So where did you wander off to earlier, Simon?"

"Oh, just here and there. No place special."

"I was disappointed when I saw you leave the meeting. I didn't know if I could convince the others without your help," Gabriel said.

"You did all right, it seems. Forty-eight mice is a large group to persuade. You did a fine job," Simon said, though his tone sounded less than enthusiastic.

Gabriel noted this immediately. "So you *will* go with us, right?"

"Yes. I said I would, didn't I? I'll listen to what the frogs have to say about finding a new home—wherever *that'll* be."

"Doesn't sound like you're excited about the idea, Simon."

Simon looked at Gabriel with weary eyes. "I have a lot on my mind right now. And Livingston's gone and… I just don't feel like talking about leaving the field."

"I understand. I love living here too, Simon. What's better than wandering about on a whim under the warm sun on a beautiful day like today?" Gabriel glanced at his friend resting in the grass. "I can't help asking again, but just where *did* you go today, Simon? I'm curious, seeing that we were in the middle of a very important meeting."

"Nowhere..."

"You had to go *somewhere*, Simon. What's the big secret?"

"There isn't a secret, Gabriel! So don't make it out to be one."

"I was just wondering what—"

"Where I go is my own business!" Simon snapped. "So stop trying to make it yours!"

Gabriel was taken aback by Simon's harsh tone. He flicked his tail and brushed back his whiskers, for an instant feeling as if he didn't know who Simon was. Simon, at the same time, realizing he might have spoken too harshly, crinkled his nose and sighed. He stood on his hind legs.

"I—I didn't mean to talk like that, Gabriel. I just..."

"Did you sneak off to the abandoned barn across the road, Simon?" Gabriel bluntly asked. "Or rather what's left of it."

"What?"

"During the meeting. Is that where you went? To the barn?"

"Why—why would I go *there*?"

Gabriel looked directly into his eyes. Simon quickly turned his head. "I saw you leave in that direction. I've had my suspicions."

Simon combed his claws over his furry body and curled his tail around a twig as he hemmed and hawed. Finally, he could no longer tolerate Gabriel's piercing gaze.

"Okay. I did. I went to the barn." His whispered words were soaked with guilt. "I had to see it, Gabriel! I really needed to. I wanted to ask you to go with me sometime, but I suspected you'd decline. That's why I left during the meeting, so you wouldn't chase after me and talk me out of it."

"Why, Simon? Why would you risk going to that dreadful place? We've never crossed the road before. Weren't you aware of the danger?" Simon looked at Gabriel, but whether fear or confidence blazed in his friend's eyes, Gabriel couldn't tell.

"I was never in any danger, Gabriel. Never. The beasts don't live there anymore. Nothing's left but a pile of blackened timber. The stench is awful!"

"I can imagine."

"Would you like to see it?"

"No! And you shouldn't again either."

Simon bowed his head. "I understand, Gabriel. But I couldn't help myself. After seeing the beasts yesterday afternoon in the woods... Then watching the one that passed by with Livingston... I—I can't explain it, Gabriel. I fear those creatures, yet they fascinate me."

Gabriel nodded. "I noticed that when we left the woods. I had to yank your tail to get you moving."

"No matter how hard I try, I can't get them out of my mind! I thought a trip to the barn might satisfy my curiosity..."

"Did it?" Gabriel challenged.

Simon didn't answer and looked away. "Let's go home, Gabriel. The shadows are growing. The sun will set soon. We shouldn't be far from home in case..."

"I know, Simon. I know."

They departed immediately and exchanged few words on the way back. Simon said a brief goodnight, and then jumped into his hole beneath the thorn bushes. Gabriel didn't feel like going inside yet and stayed out until the first stars blinked on. He wondered if Simon would be his old self tomorrow. He seemed like a stranger tonight, so wrapped up in his curiosity about the beasts. But when the shadows in the distance seemed to take on lives of their own, Gabriel abandoned his musings and rushed inside to the security of his hole and wished that the night would quickly pass.

CHAPTER EIGHT

Sleepwalking

Cold rain fell during the night, transforming sections of the field into small ponds. Rumbles of thunder reverberated miles away. In the hours before dawn, a thick blanket of white mist slowly spread across the field, nuzzling the grass blades, weed patches and the outer ring of forest trees. The threat of a more serious storm soon evaporated and the land was left in peace.

Simon stirred uneasily in his hole. He had drifted off to sleep a dozen times during the night, but the thunder constantly awakened him as if some mournful voice beckoned. He clawed at the dirt walls and jumped from one end of the hole to the other, wishing he could somehow climb out of the confines of his skin and be free. Nearly exhausted, Simon finally lay down again, groggy and disoriented. His eyelids dropped shut like clumsily drawn shades. His eyes darted back and forth in a restless dance. Two tiny claws grasped at phantoms in the air.

Then Simon popped his eyes wide open, now still and cold. A voice called to him from outdoors among the first faint traces of iron-gray light. Or was it the echo of distant thunder? Simon couldn't tell but he needed to go outside right now, away from the stuffy confinement of his hole beneath the thorn bushes. He jumped to his feet and poked his head into the gloomy dawn.

A cold white mist clung to the ground. Simon stood on his hind legs to see above it, feeling as if he were enveloped in a bank of clouds. A damp muddy smell lingered in the air and invigorated him. Simon tasted a strange exhilaration riding on the breeze. A mournful voice still called to him, though the surroundings were silent. Suddenly Simon ran through the field, sloshing through wet grass though unbothered by the biting chill. The mist fell apart as he tore through it like scissors cutting cotton. But the mist instantly mended itself when Simon passed by, swallowing him up in an ocean of billowing whitecaps.

Whether intending to or not, Simon soon arrived on the banks of the upper stream leading to the frog pond. The mist twirled above the gurgling water like somersaulting wisps of smoke. Simon glanced left with unblinking eyes in the direction of the woods, then right, towards the frog pond. Something definitely called to him. Vague and mysterious voices. He couldn't resist their allure and ran left towards the woods.

He arrived at the area where the banks grew less grassy and were littered with colorful pebbles. He remembered the day when Gabriel, Livingston and he had spent a playful afternoon near this spot. That seemed ages ago. Simon recalled the claw imprint he had secretly discovered. He vividly remembered the vicarious feeling of power it had instilled in him when standing next to it. Simon wanted to feel that way again.

Suddenly he began to scamper around the muddy ground in a fit of agitation, his nose pressed to the dirt in search of the print. The misty covering swirled overhead. Simon knew that particular print had been washed away days ago, but he needed to see it. He *had* to see it! On the verge of desperation, he carefully set his front claw into the dirt for a moment and then removed it. But Simon took no pleasure in the impression he created. As soon as he withdrew his claw, the rain-soaked soil collapsed around the imprint, leaving behind a muddy blob in the wet earth.

Simon frantically repeated the effort time and time again, growing angrier when his claw imprint wouldn't take. The young mouse desired to leave behind a record of his importance, a monument to his greatness. He *wanted* it. He *deserved* it. Simon knew in his heart that he deserved it! But in the end, all his attempts proved useless.

Simon attacked the mud ferociously, scratching the ground and kicking away the dirt with his hind feet. Then filthy and exhausted, he washed off his soiled fur on the edge of the stream, realizing he deserved nothing. He continued his journey to the woods, feeling ridiculous and insignificant.

The mist thinned out under the watchful gaze of the looming forest trees. Simon plodded on along the cold ground, shivering uncontrollably. Then before he even realized it, he had entered the woods. The trees slumped as if sleeping, bathed in black pre-dawn shadows slowly turning to gray. Simon sniffed the air, unsure why he was here though not afraid. His unblinking eyes absorbed the eerie woodscape.

Just then a snake shot out of the undergrowth and stopped short of Simon, its green and black speckled face now nose to nose with the mouse. The snake's haunting blood-red eyes transfixed Simon, as if the reptile were reading his every thought with ease. It flicked a forked tongue, startling Simon.

"Sssssssssssss… Back again, I see. Oh, but don't look so shocked, little one," it said, coiling up into a neat circle. Simon continued staring at the snake, unable to speak. "Haven't forgotten me so soon, have you? *Cat* got your tongue?"

Simon finally mustered the nerve to address his adversary. "What are you doing here?"

"Did you forget what I told you after our last visit? I am *always* here."

"What do you want?" Simon asked, still wide-eyed and unblinking.

"What do *I* want? Why am *I* here? Sssssssssssss, but my, you *are* filled with many questions this morning. And the sun hasn't even bestowed a ray of her precious light upon us yet." The snake raised its slender head and weaved back and forth, entrancing Simon with its hypnotic rhythm. "It is *you* who have come back to my home, little one. It is *you* who want things. Sssssss… Oh yes, it is all you. So tell me, mouse. Tell me what you desire."

Simon quivered, not wanting to answer but feeling forced to do so. "I want—"

"Sssssss... Tell me. Yes, tell me." The snake's blood-red eyes bore down on Simon as if scorching his mind with flames.

"I want to see—To see the b—" But Simon could say no more. He stood there like a tiny statue cast alone in the middle of a huge forest, frozen in thought and action. Trapped. Trapped inside himself.

The snake unwound its lengthy body and glided close enough to Simon to whisper in his ear. "Follow me, mouse. You don't have to answer. I *know* what you want. They are waiting for you nearby. Ssssssssssss... They have been expecting you for quite some time."

The snake slithered off into the undergrowth with hardly a sound. Though Simon couldn't see it now, he heard the snake's constant hissing and obediently followed.

Simon didn't know if he had imagined it or if it really happened, but at that instant a clap of thunder rocked the skies. Another clap followed, then another, until a fresh storm raged above the treetops. Lightning flashes lit up the forest, casting a sinister orange glow upon the trees. And though he couldn't smell any smoke or feel a burning heat, Simon believed that a fire raged a short distance away.

After what seemed a long and tiring journey, a voice commanded him to stop. Simon plopped down near the roots of a dying tree. "Where are we?" he nervously asked. But the snake was gone. Simon stood on his hind legs, alone in the middle of the black woods as a devilish storm raged above.

All at once a wall of bent and twisted shadows arose in the distance. Simon saw several pairs of green lights flitting about in the dark shapeless mass. He thought he heard growling voices and the unpleasant smacking of lips as if something were indulging in an unwholesome feast. As the shadows wavered, he slowly detected the shapes of six ragged animals. Green eyes glowed sickly in their skull sockets, and sharp yellowed fang-like teeth protruded from salivating mouths. Without a doubt, Simon knew he was in the presence of the beasts.

Yet as the lightning crackled and the thunder boomed, and the beasts finished devouring the dead animal before them, Simon gradually felt more amazed and curious at the sight rather than terrified. He watched the beasts while they finished their meal, gazing into their eerie green eyes the entire time.

Finally, the largest of the beasts cast aside the bones from the carcass then sat on its scrawny hind legs, breathing heavily. A drop of blood dripped from its mouth. The remaining five gathered around their leader in a semi-circle, then all called out to Simon in low, hideous voices.

"Come to us. We've been waiting for you." Their words sounded shrill and abrasive.

Simon approached as if being pulled by an invisible force, but he had neither the strength nor desire to run away. The beasts held a strange power over him and he knew it would be futile to resist.

"Come closer, Simon. Much closer," they chanted. "If you wish to join our ranks, then you must tell us everything we want to know. Everything!"

There was no way out. Simon had been lured to this strange world, though a part of him had once wanted to be here. Now he couldn't leave even if he wished it. He felt asleep, helplessly caught in an unfocused dream, yet he could hear the skies explode and felt the hot foul breath of the beasts burn his face. It was all too real.

"Speak!" the leader cried, its face a contortion of anger and disdain. "Speak now or I'll strike you down where you stand. Don't try my patience."

Terror seized Simon. He had to tell them everything they demanded to save his life. He again recalled the time he discovered the claw print near the stream, and now more than ever, wished he had never seen it. The creator of that marvelously horrible impression now stood before him, tormenting Simon, drawing crucial information from him against his will.

"We're leaving—We're leaving tomorrow night," Simon said in strained tones. He couldn't stop himself. "To the frog pond. Fifty of us. For information." Simon breathed heavily as his heart raced. "Then—possibly—on to a new home."

The leader snarled, wiping his red tongue across his sharp teeth. "Why a new home?"

"Because—"

"Why?"

"Because of—"

"Tell me *now*! Why?"

"Because of the beasts!" Simon cried. "Because of the beasts!"

Suddenly he told the deadly creatures every detail about the debate Gabriel had had with the other mice. He explained the mice's hatred and fear of the beasts, and their hopes for a safe new home. Simon spoke on and on and could not stop. Somehow the beasts drew the words out of him and he could not stop.

He talked and cried and pleaded before the mangy creatures, knowing in the deepest recesses of his mind that it was over. His world would never be the same. Simon realized that he had just betrayed every one of his friends back home.

The cold mists had evaporated long ago. The late morning sun shone brilliantly over the field, basking Simon in warmth and forcing him to pry open his tired eyes. He blinked uncomfortably as he lay in a patch of soft grass close to the stream. The water steadily washed over mossy rocks.

"Why am I *here*?" he wondered. "What's going on?" Simon stood. "Gabriel?"

Waves of dizziness overtook his body. Simon wobbled when he walked, sick and confused. He couldn't remember anything and wracked his brain trying to figure why he had awakened in the middle of the afternoon so far away from home. Simon tried to recall what had happened, how he got here, and then vaguely remembered poking his head out of his hole into the pre-dawn mist. That seemed ages ago, but he still couldn't determine how he had ended up here.

He thought about Gabriel and the planned meeting at the frog pond later that night. He wanted to get home quickly, fearing that his friends might be worrying about him. Simon scurried off through the drying grass and weeds, making straight for the thorn bushes beside the grassy knoll. Slowly a vague uneasiness settled over him as he ran the details of tonight's meeting through his mind. For some reason Simon didn't want to attend the gathering at the pond, even though earlier he had said he would. He didn't ever want to leave the field, though the beasts were a constant threat.

Yet at the same time, Simon had a strange inkling that even if he did leave and search for a new home, the beasts would never be far behind. They would somehow know. They would somehow always know where the mice were going. With a heavy heart, Simon made his way back to the place he had once called home.

CHAPTER NINE

A Gathering Of Frogs

Everyone assembled a few hours before sundown to bid farewell to the fifty mice departing for the frog pond. Many older couples thought Gabriel and his companions would be enthralled by stories that the frogs would tell about this new place to live—wherever it might be—and that they might never see them again. They were saddened that their close-knit community was unraveling.

"If only we could all leave together," Doris said despondently, knowing that such a dream could never come true. She and Fred were healthy enough to travel and had considered joining the group, but they were still too attached to their home near the water. Most of the other mice staying behind, however, were simply too old or too young to undertake such a long and possibly dangerous journey.

Old Thackery mouse harbored similar feelings as he stepped up onto a rock surrounded by a sea of green clover. He wanted to address the departing mice one last time in case they never returned from the frog pond. Deep inside, Thackery felt that they wouldn't.

"I believe I speak for each mouse here when I say that you will be terribly missed should you embark on finding another home," he solemnly said. The golden light of the sun gently splashed upon his gray and black fur. "Dire circumstances propel you to seek a new place to live. And should the frogs offer a better path—which in my heart I believe they will—then I only ask of you one favor."

"Anything," Gabriel said respectfully.

"After the wintry snows subside and spring is again upon our doorstep, you might consider returning to this field and take back to your new home some of the families with very young mice who can't make the journey right now," he suggested. "Though we older folks will somehow manage to live with the beasts lurking in the shadows, our young deserve a better place to grow and make their way in the world."

Many youngsters cheered Thackery, for they were also eager to leave if contending with the beasts was all they could look forward to in the coming years.

"We'll remember your words, Thackery," said Gabriel. "If one day we arrive safely at a better place, then I promise to get word back to this field. If only you could go with us now."

But there was no use in wishing for the impossible, so the mice resigned themselves to the sad facts and said their goodbyes. Even Orville the blackbird swooped down upon the scene to wish the travelers his best. He reported that a few of the birds in his territory had departed several days ago.

"I'm afraid that awful incident involving Lily and her destroyed eggs frightened away some of my less courageous companions," he said. "They flew to new grounds farther east. But most of us are staying put. It will take more than a troublesome band of beasts to run us out of our field. Besides, if we all left, who would keep an eye on you mice and report what's going on in the bigger world?"

Gabriel grinned at Orville. As much as he would like to have had a longer conversation with the bird, he knew he and his companions should leave at once before anyone started having second thoughts. Though they gave themselves plenty of travel time, they needed to reach the pond before darkness or risk unthinkable peril.

So with a heavy heart, Gabriel gave the final order to embark on their journey to the frog pond. Gabriel, Simon, Florence, Chester, Elmer and forty-five others hurried along in a tight pack like a fleeting shadow across the grass. As the late afternoon rays of the sun tinted the field gold, Orville fluttered into the air and zoomed back to his tree, squawking a final goodbye. The mice remaining behind milled about in troubled silence, wondering what the days ahead might bring.

"I'll miss our friends," Doris sniffed, as she and Fred walked slowly back home. Doris fondly recalled the many happy gatherings she and Fred had hosted upon the water's edge under a warm summery sky. Would the future ever create such wonderful times for them again?

Old Thackery mouse simply ambled back to his hole in silence. He stayed awake late into the night, a swirl of melancholy thoughts his only company.

The fifty travelers talked little along the way, swishing through the grass as softly as a whisper. They took several breaks along the way, knowing they'd reach their destination with time to spare. When the mice finally approached Livingston's blackberry bush, pangs of sorrow filled their hearts. Everyone skirted around it in somber silence, and then soon after arrived safely at the stream. The mice paused briefly to drink, greedily lapping up the chilly water. The looming cattails swayed in a gentle breeze as the first shades of twilight settled comfortably upon the land. Several stars popped out of the cobalt blue sky. The low eastern moon cast a shimmering glow across the heavens.

"Now we turn right," Gabriel said, "and follow the stream straight to the frog pond. We should arrive shortly. It wasn't very far past these cattails where Simon and I met our bullfrog friend."

"Is he a polite sort of frog?" Florence inquired with an anxious wiggle of her nose. "I never met a bullfrog up close, I'll have you know, and I certainly don't want to make a wrong first impression."

"Just be your lovable self, Florence. He may pretend to be a bit on the stern side, but overall the frog is quite a likable fellow. Didn't you think so, Simon?"

Simon, who had stayed in back of the crowd, muttered a word or two of agreement, but said nothing more. He appeared preoccupied as if he didn't want to be bothered. Gabriel sensed that something troubled his friend, but didn't voice his concern so as not to upset the others.

"If we're all ready, then let's move on," he said with a confident snap of his tail. "The frogs await us."

Gabriel led them along the water's edge, a dark wall of cattails to their left and a dusky sky encroaching upon their path. A canopy of nearby oak trees deepened the surrounding shadows. With little difficulty they arrived at the spot where Simon had fallen into the water two nights ago.

"We're losing light fast until the moon rises a bit higher, so be extra careful and stay put," Gabriel warned. "It's not easy to see where the land ends and the pond begins. You might think you're walking on solid ground, but it may turn out to be a lily pad, as Simon can attest to. No night swims this time!"

Then they waited. The mice were eager to hear of this new home, and all had expected the bullfrog to be sitting here ready to greet them. So they waited some more. And waited. And waited…

"Maybe he forgot we were coming," muttered Chester. "I had hoped for some sort of grand reception."

"We're only mice," his brother Elmer said, rolling his eyes. "What'd you expect from these frogs? A meal *and* a welcoming committee?"

"Not so loud, boys," cautioned Florence in the growing darkness. Then she turned to Gabriel. "Do you think he *did* forget?" she frantically whispered.

"No," Gabriel said. "The frog gave us his word. He'll be here. I trust him."

But as the minutes dragged by and shadows deepened, a rumbling of discontentment spread among the mice. One or two went so far as to wonder if the bullfrog had tricked Gabriel and Simon into returning here just as a joke. Or was he in league with the beasts and setting a trap? But Florence kept them in line.

"Now why would our frog do anything like that? It makes no sense. Don't be such a pessimistic pack of mice! We haven't been waiting here very long and the night's only beginning." Florence shook a tiny pink claw at the assembly as she stood her skinny frame upon a pair of thin hind legs. "We'll never find a new home with that attitude. If some of you are starting to lose your senses before we even complete our first step, then let's turn around right now and go home. We might as well put out a welcome mat for the beasts and invite them over for the next noontime forage. Only it'll be *us* on the menu. So shape up!"

Florence got down on all fours, flustered and out of breath, and nuzzled back into the stunned crowd. Gabriel had never seen his usually nervous friend so passionate before. Though he wanted to add something in support of Florence's little speech, he knew she had said it all quite nicely and merely nodded a *thank you* to her instead.

"I agree with Florence," Elmer finally said. "Let's stick to the plan. We can't start blaming Gabriel and Simon just because the frog isn't here yet. Remember, nobody was forced to go on this trip. We volunteered."

So everyone agreed to continue along the water as the weeds and grass grew ever deeper, admitting that it was unwise to give up so easily. The crickets back in the field chirped up a storm. And though hundreds of frog calls echoed in the vicinity, none of the water dwellers were yet to be found.

Suddenly a small frog leaped out of the pond and plopped directly in front of them. He was a skinny green thing with grape-like eyes, glistening in the faint rays of moonlight.

"Welcome, mice!" he said in a chipper voice. "I'm Hopper, and I've been ordered to await your arrival and take you to meet the other frogs."

Gabriel, delighted, rushed up to the frog and squeaked. "Pleased to meet you, Hopper. *Very* pleased. A few of us were getting a bit antsy when no one showed up to meet us right away."

"Oh, I've kept watch since the moment you arrived," Hopper said, "but I was ordered to observe and size up your group. One can never be too careful."

"Who gave you those orders?" Chester curiously asked.

"Our leader, of course. You'll meet him shortly."

"We look forward to it," Gabriel said. He then introduced his companions to Hopper one by one.

"What a crowd!" the frog replied. "We didn't know how many of you to expect, but we'll squeeze you into the meeting place somehow. The others are anxious to hear your story. It's not often we get news from the outside. We frogs tend to stick around our water hole and wait for word from the field to come to us. But enough chatter. Plenty of time for that later. I must take you to the meeting place where everyone is patiently waiting. Follow me. There is much to discuss tonight!"

In a flash, Hopper sprang into the air and took a great leap forward. The mice scurried after him, following his shiny green body in the moonlight. They traveled for a few minutes, shifting their direction like a flock of birds from time to time as Hopper abruptly veered left or right without warning.

"My, that Hopper *is* a swift and nimble frog," Florence whispered to Violet, a younger mouse running next to her. "I hope I have the strength to keep up."

"Certainly his mother *named* him properly," Violet replied with a giggle.

After trekking through a forest of cattails over muddy and mossy ground, the mice arrived at a small clearing that offered a wide view of the frog pond. Dark still waters captured the silvery reflection of the rising full moon through the surrounding trees. Blankets of green lily pads covered some areas of the pond, and most of its shoreline was packed with cattails that shot out of the water like pillars. The remains of a fallen tree lay half submerged in the water, with abundant weeds growing along its sides, having wrapped themselves securely about the trunk over time to claim it for the pond. And there in the midst of this watery and dreamlike haven were the frogs.

Hundreds of frogs, all especially gathered for this most unusual meeting with the mice. Some perched on the lily pads while others squatted on the tree trunk. Several observed from among the thick cattails along the edge. A few lazily floated in the water with only their bulging eyes peering above the surface to witness the proceedings.

Hopper escorted the mice along the fallen tree so they could look down upon the croaking community. Faint moon glow illuminated the frogs' glistening green bodies in shades of emerald, olive and lime. Directly below the fallen tree, on top of an enormous lily pad and at the center of attention, sat their leader, the very same bullfrog Gabriel and Simon had previously met. He smiled broadly because the two mice had returned.

"So we meet again, young mice," the frog said in a voice as deep as the darkness. "I am pleased you have taken me up on my offer. I trust you had no trouble finding our meeting grounds?"

"None at all," Gabriel replied. "Hopper proved to be an excellent guide."

The other frogs croaked in appreciation of the compliment till the bullfrog quieted them. "Thank you for your kind words," he said. "And since you have returned and appear to be who you claim, I feel I can now entrust you with an important piece of information—*my* name. I am Greenback, and I have been chosen as leader of our small community."

"We appreciate your trust," Gabriel said, whereupon he exchanged a few words with Greenback about the mice's trip to the pond. Then with the introductions and pleasantries out of the way, Gabriel asked the two questions that were foremost on everyone's mind. "Where exactly is this new home you spoke of the other day? And how do we get there?"

"The answers to those questions and others will be given at once," Greenback said. "But it will be the job of another to do so." Greenback scanned the audience and finally pointed to another frog. "Long Legs. You joined us in the pond most recently. Please come over here and explain to our new friends exactly where you used to live."

"With pleasure, Greenback!" the frog announced, eager to have the spotlight to himself.

He leaped off his lily pad and swam under water, then emerged onto a smaller pad floating next to Greenback's. All eyes were on Long Legs.

"It was over two full moons ago that I was brought to this place," the frog said. He sat with his hind feet widely splayed out upon the pad so that his knees nearly touched the sides of his face. "Several of my family and friends accompanied me. You see, some of us living here now used to reside in a different pond. It was much smaller than this one, though charming and wonderful nonetheless." Long Legs' eyes lit up with affection for his old home. "That pond is situated in a lovely garden near a magnificent stone house upon lush green lawns, surrounded by pine trees and maple trees and blooming flowers of every color imaginable. And the people there! All sorts of every age, coming and going and thoroughly busy." Long Legs saw how the mice lingered on his every word. Even some of the frogs native to this pond appeared fascinated by his tale, though they had heard it many times before. "And surrounding this huge house that lies away in the east is a stone wall with a large white metal gate in front. I saw this gate up close once."

"When?" Violet whispered.

"On the very day I was carried through it in a bucket of water, never to return."

"Who—who put you in that bucket of water?" Florence asked in shock. "And why?" The tail at the end of her skinny body bobbed up and down as she excitedly pranced about. "Why, if someone tried to place *me* in a bucket of water, well, I'd, I'd… Well, I wouldn't *like* it, *that's* for sure!"

Violet attempted to calm Florence as Chester tried to keep from laughing at her antics. "How long did you live in that other pond before you were moved?" he managed to ask with a straight face.

"I had lived there all my life. But don't get the wrong impression," Long Legs explained. "It's not as horrible as it sounds. You see, that pond is much smaller than this one, and it grew quite crowded after a time. So one fine sunny morning last spring, two individuals in the household strolled down to the garden pond with a metal pail and a couple of small nets. One stood tall with white hair and wrinkles on his skin. The other was quite young, always smiling and laughing, with a face full of red dots and a wide toothy grin. They seemed to be having a swell time."

"What exactly did they do with that—that *bucket*?" Florence asked, trying to remain calm.

"It seems they also thought there were too many frogs in the pond, so they dipped their nets into the water, carefully scooped some of us out, and plopped us into the bucket that they had already filled with pond water." Long Legs expanded his chest and croaked. "Then they carried the bucket across the lawn and through the front gate and set it inside one of their numerous metal contraptions on wheels. We were taken to *this* pond and gently dumped into the water next to those cattails over there, and left on our own to find new homes."

"The nerve of them," Elmer said. "Taking you from your home and throwing you in this pond. How rude!" Just as Elmer said this, he caught a glimpse of Greenback's roving eye and swallowed hard. "Not that there's anything wrong with living *here* though," he quickly added before hiding in back of the crowd.

"Nothing at all," Long Legs assured them. "In fact, I have much more room to swim now and many more companions to chat with. This is a wonderful place to live. But the point of my story is that the place where I came from is a safe haven. The people living there don't bother a soul and the grounds are always maintained. And because of the stone wall surrounding the property, there's not a predator to bother anything from a bird to a squirrel—to a mouse."

Gabriel's eyes lit up in hope as the other mice chattered with excitement. "You mean other mice already live there?"

"I've met plenty of them near the garden pond. Some were very good friends of mine," said Long Legs. "So if you mice are attempting to flee from some beasts as Greenback has informed me, well then, there wouldn't be a more suitable place to escape to than that lovely estate in the east."

It didn't take much beyond Long Legs' dazzling description to convince the mice where to seek out a new home. Lush and beautiful surroundings. A stone wall encircling the property. Other mice already live there. The estate in the east sounded like perfection. Gabriel and his companions couldn't have asked for anything more. Before Long Legs could continue with his account of his old home, the mice spontaneously agreed to go there as soon as possible.

Simon, though less enthusiastic than the others, appeared to play along. Then a simple matter struck him. "Excuse me," he said, trying to talk above the din. But nobody heard him. "Excuse me!" Simon repeated, raising his squeaky voice. The others finally took notice.

"You have something to say?" Greenback asked, staring at Simon. "Then step forward and speak."

Simon uncomfortably inched up to the edge of the tree trunk so that he could see his reflection in the moonlit water below. He quickly backed away a step. "Not meaning to put a damper on the situation, but… How do we get there? We don't even know where this estate is. We could get lost—or worse. Maybe we shouldn't leave after all and return to our field instead."

The other mice moaned in disappointment. What could Simon be thinking, some of them wondered. Others ignored his suggestion and attributed it to last-minute jitters.

"Nonsense!" Greenback piped up. "There's no need to abandon your plan before you even attempt it. I've taken care of the details. You'll have no trouble finding this estate in the east. Trust me."

With that, Greenback emitted an enormously loud croak that echoed across the pond. Suddenly a large blackbird fluttered onto the scene and alighted on the highest point of the tree trunk. The moonlight illuminated his glistening black body, highlighting traces of ruby red on the tip of his head that seemed to appear and disappear depending on his position.

"Everyone, I'd like you to meet Wilbur, a friend of ours here at the pond. He resides in one of the nearby trees and has offered to help you in your quest."

The mice introduced themselves and soon learned that Wilbur had agreed to fly to the estate on their behalf. He would ask one of the mice living there to travel back to the pond and serve as a guide for Gabriel and his friends.

"I would have left yesterday," Wilbur said, "but Greenback insisted that I wait until you were sure about going through with the plan."

"I didn't want to invite a guide mouse all this way if you didn't really want to move to the estate," Greenback explained.

"We're *all* eager to go," Elmer said, amid nods of approval. "And the sooner, the better!"

"Then it's settled," Greenback announced.

The bullfrog nodded to Wilbur, and the blackbird immediately took to flight without as much as a goodbye. He was off to the estate to find a guide. Greenback, in the meantime, dismissed the gathering of frogs and mice, informing Gabriel and his friends that they were once again free to spend the night along the edge of the pond.

"When will our guide get here?" Violet asked excitedly. "I do so much want to see this new home."

"Whoever Wilbur finds will travel throughout the night, so he probably won't arrive till late tomorrow morning at the earliest," Greenback guessed. "So settle down and get all the rest you can. You'll need it for your journey ahead. Now good night," he said, then dove into the water and disappeared.

The other frogs immediately jumped into the pond too, creating a series of splashes as if a fistful of stones had been cast high into the air before dropping into the water below. Moments later the meeting place was abandoned, the water's surface now still as ice. Moonlight filtered down through the nearby trees as legions of dark cattails stood guard. Cricket chirps and frog calls again pulsed against the backdrop of night.

"Greenback seems like an awfully nice frog," Florence remarked softly as she followed the others off the tree trunk and back onto solid ground.

"I think so too," Violet said.

Others echoed her sentiments. Simon said nothing.

Gabriel agreed. "I believe everything will work out for the best. But now we should get some rest." He led the group along the water's edge toward a clump of cattails. "I think that after today's excitement I could sleep till sunrise, and the wildest storm couldn't wake me."

And he did just that.

CHAPTER TEN

Betrayal

Forty-nine mice slumbered amid the night noises along the pond—the thin splash of a solitary fish jumping to catch the stars, or the gentle rustle of cattails upon a whispering breeze. Rushing waters of the nearby stream gurgled over mossy rocks, while the ever-present symphony of crickets and frogs played invisibly in the background.

One mouse, however, struggled with bouts of fitful sleep. Simon tossed and turned on his bed of thick grass. At times he unconsciously scratched at the ground with his pinkish claws, shredding the grass blades as if they were bits of newspaper. Then an army of dreams invaded, attacking his mind with an endless stream of vacant voices and shadowy images—dreary, lifeless and lonely. The dreams pelted his mind like icy raindrops.

Slowly, however, the sounds and images grew milder and brighter. Voices beckoned to him from afar and Simon wanted to respond. He felt an irresistible desire to be a part of them.

Then he was. Simon dreamed he was running between a wall of grass and a river of water, then rushing through a forest of green and fragrant trees, all the while trying to discover the source of these beautiful images and sounds. Laughter and music drew him, and a display of intense colors he had never known existed flashed wildly in the air. He wanted to learn where it all began and what it all meant, so he ran faster and faster as the trees grew taller and closer together, blotting out the stars.

More running, and even more still, until Simon felt tired and out of breath. Suddenly he found himself in a clearing. Trees encircled him like sentries as stars blazed above. Those beautiful voices he had sought swirled around him, emanating from a large black boulder in the middle of the clearing. The voices called to Simon and he approached.

A darkness blacker than night itself slowly engulfed him at the same time. The pleasant music and voices gradually turned shrill and grating, stinging his ears. The huge boulder, now growing and wavering and moving in every direction, seemed to be alive. Soon the huge dark object dissolved into smaller segments, six black undulating pieces, each with legs and tails and glowing green eyes. The harsh noises transformed into hisses and vicious laughter. Haggard faces baring sharp teeth surrounded Simon, approaching closer and closer in the inky night.

Simon tried to scream and run away, but his lungs burned and his legs felt like lead. The beasts spun around him in a fiery cyclone. Simon felt dizzy and lost in time. He started to speak, unable to stop, answering every question they pummeled him with till his head felt ready to burst. Simon chattered away, unable to focus on their faces, hardly hearing his own words. But a small part of his conscious mind did understand, and Simon realized he was telling the beasts about the meeting with the frogs. He described the new home at the estate in the east and the mice's impending journey there.

The beasts howled in glee at each bit of information. Simon grew more terrified but he couldn't stop talking. Some sinister force compelled him to tell everything he knew until there was nothing more to say. Then the small mouse fainted and collapsed on the cold ground.

Simon awoke from his horrible dream as the first gray light of dawn seeped into the eastern sky. He lay on the ground, dead tired, nearly unable to move. Simon thought he should wake Gabriel to discuss the strange details of his dream. He realized that he had been rather distant lately and felt bad for cutting Gabriel out of his life. Maybe asking for his opinion about the dream might go a long way towards patching things up.

Simon got to his feet then noticed something unusual. A chill ran through to his heart. He was no longer in a bed of grass near the cattails along the edge of the frog pond. Instead, Simon had been sleeping on a stony patch of soil a few feet from the stream just outside the edge of the woods. What frightened Simon even more was the scattering of claw prints over the soil near the spot where he had slept.

Simon's heart beat wildly. He shook like a leaf caught in a blustery autumn wind as the awful truth struck him. He had not been dreaming last night. He had actually met with the beasts inside the dark woods. Somehow they had summoned him in his sleep and Simon had willingly gone to their abode. One of them must have carried him back here after he had fainted, Simon guessed. Worst of all, Simon now recalled that he had revealed every last detail to the beasts. *Everything!* The frogs. The late night meeting. Their planned flight to freedom. The beasts knew it all.

Simon broke down and cried.

Simon raced back to the pond, tearing through bundles of cattails and tufts of grass till he found his bed. The other mice still slept soundly, and the night din around the pond had quieted. Simon lay down and closed his eyes, trembling and cold. He felt sick and empty inside. He pretended to sleep until the others stirred.

But deep down, Simon hoped the morning sun would never rise. He wanted to close his eyes forever so he wouldn't have to face his friends. If they knew what he had done, they would never call him a friend again. Pangs of guilt pricked Simon like hot needles. No matter how or why it happened, he realized that he had endangered them all. Simon was certain their plans were in peril and feared that all was lost.

CHAPTER ELEVEN

The Journey Begins

Hopper landed smack in the middle of the mice without warning as they enjoyed a late breakfast. Many shot into the nearby grass for cover, believing they were under attack, but the frog gradually coaxed them back into the open.

"You must follow me at once," Hopper said.

"What's going on?" Chester asked, hiding behind a leafy weed patch, annoyed that his meal had been disturbed.

"Greenback has summoned everyone to the gathering place for another meeting," announced Hopper as the mice returned to their meals after the false alarm.

"Perhaps signaling your arrival might be in order next time," Florence suggested with a raised eye as she poked her head through a tuft of grass. "Good manners *are* important. Now what exactly is all the fuss about, Hopper? Why another meeting so soon?"

"Greenback wants to address your group one last time before you leave. Your guide from the estate arrived only moments ago."

"That's wonderful news!" Gabriel said, scurrying towards the frog. "I didn't expect him so soon."

"He is here nonetheless," said Hopper. "So snap to it if you want to meet him."

Gabriel signaled for everyone to gather round. "Let's not keep Greenback waiting. He's gone to a lot of trouble to assist us, and there are still many details to sort out before our journey."

The mice abandoned their half-eaten morsels and nearly climbed over one another to get close to Hopper. The frog was overwhelmed by their eagerness.

"What did our guide say?" one of the mice asked.

"Can we leave at once?" Elmer added amid the jostling bodies and waving tails.

"All of your questions will be answered in due time if you'll follow me," Hopper said to the encroaching mice. "Just don't get *too* close please. I need my leaping space."

With that, the sleek frog bounded off in a flash with the furry and squeaky throng in pursuit. Though at times Hopper got well ahead of them, the mice remembered the way to the gathering place and arrived with little difficulty.

All the frogs were again seated on the lily pads or among the cattails as the mice scrambled along the fallen tree. Standing there to greet them was a light chocolate-colored mouse not much older than Gabriel, but who appeared taller and larger compared to the others. Gabriel assumed he would be their guide.

"Good morning," Greenback said while seated atop his lily pad directly below the half-submerged tree. "I hope your stay last night proved to be restful, because you'll definitely need that rest to undertake the journey ahead."

The mice, except for Simon, assured their host that the evening had been a pleasant one. They thanked Greenback many times over for his hospitality. Then the frog introduced them to their guide from the estate. His name was Edmund and he had lived behind the walls of the estate all his life.

"I couldn't imagine living anywhere else," he said. "There is plenty of food and so much space to explore. And best of all, we're safe from predators." The other mice didn't doubt that fact for a moment judging from Edmund's large size.

"Less running around, I suppose," Florence whispered to Violet. "I'm sure we'll plump up in no time without having to constantly worry about beasts sneaking up on us."

"What if we don't like it there?" Simon asked to the consternation of many.

"You're free to return home, of course," Edmund said, puzzled by the question. "But I guarantee you'll have no regrets." He painted a picture of life at the estate even more marvelous than what Long Legs had described. "There's rarely a care in our world behind the stone walls. And none of those creatures Wilbur told me about."

Elmer sat on his hind legs to question Edmund, his face scrunched up with uncertainty. "Excuse me, but do *none* of your friends object to more mice coming back to live with you?" After listening to Edmund's wonderful account, Elmer found it difficult to imagine that others at the estate would want to share their treasured lifestyle.

"Each of you is wholeheartedly welcome to live at the estate." Edmund's words rang with sincerity. "In fact, we eagerly look forward to your company. Though we have nearly everything we could hope for at our home, there is *one* item we lack."

"I knew there must be a catch," a mouse in the back uttered, brimming with skepticism.

Edmund calmed his doubts with a smile. "What we lack are tales of the outside world. You mice could provide exactly that—a whole drove of exciting stories to take us through the cold dreary winter. Though from time to time we get an occasional nugget of news from a passing bird, it would be wonderful to hear stories of the wild from other mice. Your group will be quite popular upon arrival. Take my word for it."

"We'll be happy to share our stories," Gabriel said. "That's more than a fair exchange for new living quarters. But I don't think anybody here is really interested in being a celebrity of sorts. We're just plain field mice when you get right down to it."

"Speak for yourself, Gabriel," said Florence, while combing her claws gently through her fur and batting her eyelids. "I won't object in the least if some mature and sophisticated gentlemouse should fawn all over me because of my scintillating storytelling." She cast a questioning gaze at Edmund. "Tell me that you *do* have some mature and sophisticated gentlemice living at the estate?"

Gabriel found Florence's behavior amusing, but tried not to giggle too loudly. He noticed that Violet grinned as well when he glanced her way. Gabriel smiled at Violet and was glad when she smiled back. For the first time he noticed how pretty her eyes were, the color of green clover on a dewy morning. Violet's light brown fur was tinged with a hint of strawberry red now visible in the morning sun.

Edmund continued to answer a downpour of questions from the mice concerning details about the estate and the journey to it. Some questions he answered two and three times in various forms till he felt more worn out from talking than from his overnight trip to the pond. Greenback listened as patiently as he could from his lily pad, but finally interrupted the conversation with a loud croak.

"Are you mice just about finished?" he asked, hoping to hurry them along yet not wanting to appear rude. "My, but you are the most inquisitive creatures I've ever met. As presider over this now overly-long gathering, let me lay the final question upon the water. *Do you mice wish to return to the estate with Edmund?*"

"Of course we do!" Florence squeaked after eyeing her companions for their approval.

"Without a doubt!" added Elmer.

"And as soon as possible!" said many of the others.

Gabriel simply nodded with a smile, happy to see that his companions enthusiastically agreed in the end without any prompting from him.

As a brief celebration commenced along the shores of the pond, Simon trudged off by himself to think. He curled up next to a tower of cattails as the sounds of the festivities drifted by. Deep in his heart he yearned to go to the estate, but after last night he doubted that they would ever make it.

The journey to their new home began at mid-afternoon after Edmund had rested from his trek to the pond. Before everyone departed, Edmund familiarized Gabriel and a few of the other mice with the route they would take to the estate. If all went well, Edmund guessed that the travelers would arrive shortly before nightfall. He didn't foresee any major problems as the terrain was relatively flat most of the way and quite deserted.

"That's good news," Gabriel said. "The last thing we need is something keeping an eye on our progress. I want this trip to proceed with as little fanfare as possible."

Then the mice said goodbye to Greenback and the other frogs, thanking them repeatedly for their abundant hospitality and for assistance in finding a new home. Though their stay at the pond was a short one, some of the mice had grown attached to the wet and weedy surroundings.

"If you ever visit the frog pond at the estate," Long Legs said, "be sure to say hello to everyone. Tell them about our new life here. Many will be interested in knowing how we're doing."

"Consider it done," Gabriel said.

Greenback had the final word. "And should any of you mice travel this way again, please feel free to stop by for a chat or for more frogly advice. We have plenty to spare. Now farewell and safe traveling!"

With that, Greenback leaped into the air and splashed into the pond like a rock. The other frogs followed his lead in bunches, and after several seconds of splattering water and choppy waves, the pond lay still like green glass.

"Well, I guess that's that," said Gabriel flatly. "No fuss. No commotion. Just what we asked for. Now the rest is up to us." He scanned the concerned yet excited faces of his friends, feeling the weight of their collective gaze. Though Edmund would serve as their guide to the estate, Gabriel knew only too well that they had chosen *him* as their leader. He hoped he was up to the task and wouldn't betray their trust. "Let's go!" he said confidently. "There's no turning back now. Edmund, lead on."

So began their march across the field under the sweltering summer sun. The mice spoke little to each other that first hour. The uneasy stillness was broken only by the rustling of dry grass and the rhythmic chirping of crickets. The occasional caw of a distant crow only seemed to magnify the strained silence.

Not until the frog pond appeared as a small green dot in the west did the mice begin to relax and let down their guard. Once or twice they even paused for a few moments to run around the field and chase each other or look for food, squeaking with delight. A warm breeze sent white billowing clouds sailing overhead like vast ships on a blue sea. With anxiety lessening, the group enjoyed their little adventure more and more. Except Simon. He rested under the shade of some thistle, deep in thought. Florence noticed him as the other mice frolicked in the grass and approached.

"Why don't you join the rest of us, Simon? Not sick, are you?"

"No, Florence," he replied with some effort. "I just don't feel much like running around today. I'd rather we moved on and reached the estate before nightfall. There'll be plenty of time for fun and games later."

"We'll get there soon enough, Simon. Just enjoying our time together on this little trip, is all. It's not every day we search out a new home." Florence examined Simon with a questioning eye and a wiggle of her nose. "You're *sure* you're not ill? You've been awfully quiet today."

"You haven't been spying on me, have you, Florence?"

"Of course not! Don't be silly. It's just that I get concerned about you younger mice from time to time. If something's bothering you, I'm more than happy to listen and maybe help you sort matters out." Florence looked at Simon with her head tilted to one side, holding her tail in her pinkish claws.

Simon tried to smile and put his concerned friend at ease. "I do have a lot on my mind lately, Florence, but I'm really not in the talking mood."

"No running. No talking. I completely understand," she said. "I'll bet you're still upset about Livingston. After all, you and Gabriel were his best friends. I miss him too. So you take all the time you want to sort things out, Simon."

"Thank you. I will."

"Now I'll rejoin the others, unless, that is, you'd rather have me stay here. We don't *have* to talk. I can think quietly and keep you company at the same time."

Simon scratched the ground and took an impatient breath. "I really *do* wish to be left alone, Florence."

"Well, okay then," she replied, dropping her tail. "I'll scurry off and leave you to your thoughts. But try not to worry *too* much. Those beasts may have gotten Livingston, but we'll be free of them soon. You'll see."

At the mention of the beasts, Simon's eyes widened in anger. He swept a claw through the grass with such force that he startled Florence. "Why'd you have to mention the beasts? I don't want to hear anything about them again—*ever*! Do you hear me? Not ever!"

Simon glowered at Florence for a moment and then shot off into the field, leaving her puzzled and saddened and alone. Gabriel found Florence a few moments later, shaking. She uneasily explained the incident with Simon.

"He looked so unlike his usual self, Gabriel. Mad at the world, almost. If he hadn't run off, I *would* have out of fear," she admitted.

"I'm sorry this happened, Florence, but it confirms my suspicions of late. Simon *has* been acting strangely." Gabriel paced uneasily beneath the thistle dotted with purple flowers. "I hoped his behavior would return to normal once we began this journey."

"When we reach our new home he can start fresh," Florence said hopefully. "Simon can put all thoughts about the beasts and what they did to Livingston behind him."

"I hope that's all it takes, Florence, but I'm not so sure," he said, punctuating his words with a disheartened sigh. "Let's keep this little episode between us, okay? No sense in spoiling everyone else's good spirits."

"Okay, Gabriel."

"If you would, Florence, ask Edmund to start rounding up the others in a few moments. We'd better be on our way shortly. I'll find Simon."

Gabriel then sprinted out of sight, leaving Florence more worried than ever. She turned to rejoin the others, muttering discouraging words to herself as she searched for Edmund.

They had continued on for some time when at last they neared a small creek winding lazily through the field. Edmund happily announced that it marked the halfway point of their journey.

"The terrain beyond isn't much different, but it'll seem easier because we're getting closer to our destination. So give yourselves a pat on the back for getting this far," he said. "You deserve it."

"Edmund, how do we get across the creek?" a young mouse named Lewis asked. "The water looks way too deep to walk through."

"Or to swim across!" Florence quickly added. "You don't intend for us to *swim* across, do you, Edmund? Because I'll tell you right now, we field mice are *not* swimmers. You mice living behind the walls at the estate may have taken to the water, but *we* have not. I'd just as soon sit here till you gnaw down a tree limb to lay across the creek for a bridge before I'll attempt a swim across *that* water!"

Edmund waited patiently for Florence to conclude. "We are not going to swim across, Florence. The current is too strong and would sweep us away."

"That's good to hear."

"There is *another* way. You were on to something, Florence, when you mentioned a bridge."

"Oh, I *was*?" she said excitedly, and then suddenly her mood blackened again. "You don't intend for us to *gnaw* down a tree limb, do you, Edmund? Because I'll tell you right now, we field mice are *not*—"

"Florence!" Gabriel shouted, with a stern eye aimed her way. "Let Edmund finish."

"Oh… Very well then," she said, a bit miffed. "Please continue, Edmund, and we'll just listen here quietly like a bunch of stones." She poked her nose in the air and looked away.

"There's nothing to be apprehensive about, Florence," Edmund continued. "I promise that you won't have to swim across water or gnaw down tree limbs or do *any* such cumbersome task. The only thing we need to do is *walk*. Down the stream a short way near a patch of wild strawberries is a series of small rocks stretching across the water like a bridge. We can walk over them to the other side. That's how I made it over to this side on my way *from* the estate."

"That doesn't sound bad at all," Violet said. "Though I can't imagine what you would have done if those rocks weren't there."

"Edmund would have had to search up and down the stream for a different path on his way over here," Gabriel said. "Who knows how much longer we'd have had to travel in that case."

"You're very fortunate to have a nearly straight path to the estate," Edmund told them. "So let's move on. I'll cross first."

Edmund guided them to the patch of wild strawberries a short distance south along the creek. To the mice's disappointment, the delectable pieces of fruit they imagined feasting upon had been eaten

74

by others long ago. Since there wasn't time to dawdle anyway, Edmund led them to the edge of the bubbling water to show them where to cross.

Five flat rocks were strewn across the creek, but spaced closely enough so that the mice could walk across them with little difficulty. They were dry on top, having baked in the sun all afternoon. The only minor difficulty was a slightly wider gap between the fourth and fifth rocks. Here each mouse would have to make a running leap across to avoid the rush of water below that could easily carry someone their size away should one of them misstep. Before anyone could raise an objection, Edmund scurried over the rocks as casually as could be, jumping over the gap without even thinking about it, and then scrambled up a slight incline in the bank on the other side.

"See! No problem. Just continue across without stopping or thinking about falling and you'll have no trouble."

"Easy for you to say," Florence muttered to herself.

Even some of the others scoffed at Edmund under their breath for appearing so boastful and unafraid. He was a much larger and stronger mouse, after all, and the task would naturally seem less daunting to him. Gabriel sensed worry and uneasiness creeping through the group and feared a major delay would result if their jitters got the best of them. So in a flash, Gabriel raced to the water's edge, then charged across the creek, rock by rock—even jumping between the forth and fifth ones as if he had done it a dozen times before—till he stood beside Edmund on the other side. Gabriel grinned wildly and waved his tail with pride.

"Edmund's right!" he boasted a little. "There's nothing to it. Really kind of fun." He waved for the others to cross. "Hurry now, but one at a time. We don't want to be stuck here till dark."

No one argued that point, but still some of the mice were reluctant to proceed. Simon, though, who wanted nothing more than to get to the estate and end this dreary journey, ignored the grumbling of his companions and pushed to the front. Without a word, he dashed across the water with ease, and reached the other side as casually as stepping out of his mouse hole. Some thought Simon performed the task with even more confidence than Gabriel.

"Good for you, Simon!" Gabriel congratulated him. "I knew you could do it."

"Now see if you can get the rest of those slowpokes to do the same," Simon coolly complained. He sat in the grass and said nothing more.

Gabriel ignored the remark, but was grateful because Simon's initiative had a positive effect on the others. On the opposite side of the creek, the mice appeared more confident as several approached the water's edge. Then one by one they began to cross, some slowly and deliberately, others quite swiftly once they determined that traversing the bridge of stones wasn't such a difficult maneuver after all.

Florence crossed last, and though still feeling ill at ease, she refused to show it. She took to the rocks at last—ONE, TWO, THREE, FOUR (*Ready? Set? Jump!*) FIVE—then onto the bank, all without a single hitch. Everyone cheered after she safely crossed. Florence beamed with pride.

"Well done," Edmund said, glancing at the sun as it edged steadily to the west. "That didn't take as much time as it could have, but still more than I wished. We've slowed up a bit, so let's travel a good distance without a stop before searching for a bite to eat."

Everyone settled down after congratulating one another. But as they prepared to move out, a terrible cry arose on a warm wind from the west. The shrill call shattered the lazy late afternoon stillness and chilled the hearts of the mice.

"What in the field was *that*?" Violet whispered, looking at Gabriel for an explanation.

"Whatever it was, it didn't sound very pleasant to me," Elmer whispered.

Gabriel wondered with the rest of them. He noticed Simon facing the west, looking like a statue. "Perhaps it was a bird of some sort," he said with little conviction.

"Or perhaps not…" Chester quietly added.

The sun continued to beat down in the ensuing silence. Shadows lengthened, stretching thinly towards the east. A dry breeze offered little comfort from the heat.

"Let's get out of here," Florence urged the others with a tremor in her voice. "We've wasted enough time."

"Florence is right," Edmund said. "Follow me."

Instantly the mice dashed silently through the field like the shadow of a passing cloud, leaving the babbling creek and the harrowing cries behind.

The swiftly passing minutes stretched into an hour, then nearly two, before the group of tired mice felt they could travel no longer. Finally, when happening upon a tangle of blackberry bushes growing among a thicket of wild peppergrass, Edmund gave the order to stop. Soon the fifty-one mice feasted on the delicious sweet treat as the sun dipped closer to the western horizon.

"What luck having found these berries!" Chester exclaimed. "I feel like I haven't eaten for days."

"Luck had nothing to do with it," Edmund said. "Wilbur spotted these blackberry bushes while flying over to the estate and guided me to the frog pond this way. We decided it would make a perfect place for us to stop before completing the final leg of our journey."

"Get your fill, everyone," Gabriel advised as he reached for a stem of the bush low to the ground. "Where to from here, Edmund?" he asked between mouthfuls.

"Straight on till we approach a huge boulder sitting half buried in the field," he said. "Just beyond the rock is a rotting hollow log surrounded by weeds."

"Is *that* near the estate?" Lewis asked.

"Close to it. When we reach the log there'll be a tall willow tree nearby. We'll gather at the base of the tree. From that spot you'll see the gray stone wall of the estate snaking across the grass. It'll be good to see again," Edmund said. "As much as I enjoyed taking part in this exciting adventure, I miss my home. We'll get there soon enough and then relax for a spell."

Florence piped up. "Tell us more about our new home, Edmund. Especially the gardens. Our field is filled with assorted wild flowers, but I'm sure they can't compare to the beautiful and fragrant blossoms I've imagined growing at the estate."

"There are several gardens carefully tended to behind the walls, Florence, with an uncountable variety of flowers blooming from springtime through the fall. And there are lots of leafy trees and stretches of lush green lawns that you never thought could exist." Edmund gushed with enthusiasm. "Of course, there's the frog pond too, and a well and several rock gardens. And just so you won't feel too homesick, there are even a few sections of grass near the back wall that have been left to grow wild just like in this field. And I'm only describing the sections of the estate away from the main dwelling. My friends and I stay away from the human activity most of the time since there is so much room elsewhere. Except for on *one* particular day. But you'll find out about that soon enough."

"This place sounds as big as our field," Elmer declared.

"One might think," Edmund agreed. "None of us mice living there have ever longed for more room. In fact—"

But Edmund didn't get a chance to finish his sentence. Another ear-piercing cry sounded from the west, though much closer than the last time. The mice froze as the noise grabbed their senses like twisting vines, chilling them to the bone. Each knew that this particular cry was *not* from a bird.

"It sounded awfully close this time," said Gabriel. "And if I'm not mistaken, I believe I heard more than one voice mixed up in that cry."

"As much as I hate to admit it," Violet said, "I think you're right, Gabriel."

Gabriel wasn't mistaken. A few seconds later, several more frightful cries filled the air, and then all went quiet. Shadows lengthened considerably across the field as the sun inched its way closer to setting. Though no one dared to say so aloud, all knew that the beasts were stirring somewhere in the field, closer than they dared to imagine.

"No time to lose!" Gabriel said quickly but calmly. "Let's move as fast as we can. I don't know how it's possible, but I fear the danger that we were fleeing is again on our tails. Lead on, Edmund."

The mice anxiously darted through grass and weeds and along wild flowers and bare patches of ground as twilight cast its first dreamy shadows upon the earth. None dared to look behind. Upon a rise in the ground they caught their first glimpse of the large willow tree in the distance, and beyond that, the vague outline of a gray stone wall lying upon the land like a sleeping snake. Home. But it still loomed a long way off.

"We should be approaching the hollow log shortly," Edmund assured them. Thin tinny screeches echoed in the distance from time to time, getting closer and sharper. "I've got an idea," Edmund said, stopping suddenly.

"What are you doing?" Florence squeaked. "We have to keep moving! We all know it's the beasts that are following us, though I can't figure out how they discovered we were going this way."

"You can speculate about that later. Right now we need to split into two groups," Edmund instructed. "Gabriel, lead half of the mice that way past the rock just ahead till you get to the log. I'll take the rest round the opposite way and meet you there. We'll move faster and maybe confuse any pursuer."

Edmund and Gabriel swiftly divided the company and scattered in opposite directions, with many of the mice wondering which group would be attacked first. No sooner had they departed when the cries of the beasts filled the dusky air. They closed in like wildfire.

"I don't think I like this!" Violet said. She ran next to Florence, her heart pounding. Violet was amazed at how fast her older friend could move.

"Just don't *think*, Violet. Run, run and run some more!"

Gabriel, who led this group, noticed Simon lagging behind and so inched closer to Chester. "I'm placing you in charge. Get everyone to the log, Chester, and I'll catch up with you shortly! Simon needs my help."

"All right, Gabriel. But don't tarry! Time's against us."

As Chester and the rest of the group passed by, Gabriel found Simon standing stone-still under the emerging stars, staring fixedly in the direction of the cries. He looked at Simon nose to nose.

"What's the matter with you, Simon? We've got to move now or we'll be killed!"

But Simon remained in a hypnotic state and barely noticed his friend. "Go on, Gabriel. Don't worry about me. I'll be all right."

"I'm not leaving without you!" Gabriel insisted. But he knew he didn't have the time or patience to reason with Simon. He needed to act fast. "You're coming with me, Simon, like it or not!"

Suddenly, Gabriel grabbed Simon's tail with his sharp claws and yanked it with all his might. Simon screamed in agony and twisted round, hissing and threatening his friend. Gabriel, pleased that his stunt had produced its intended effect, dashed towards the rock with Simon chasing madly after him.

"I'll get you for that!" Simon cried. He would have gladly scratched Gabriel if he could have laid his claws on him.

"You're too slow to ever catch me!" Gabriel taunted, rounding the great boulder that stood like a gray giant in the twilight. Simon continued to vent his anger during the chase.

Finally they saw the hollow log ahead. The other mice in their group were filing inside through a tiny hole in the bottom at the far end. A forest of weeds sprouted around it. Gabriel arrived at the entrance first and waited for Simon to catch up. As he did, Gabriel noticed that his friend's anger had evaporated and that Simon was his old self again, at least for a while.

"Are you okay?" Gabriel asked.

"I guess…" Simon said, out of breath. "Thanks."

As the two slipped inside the log, Edmund and his group arrived. They also scrambled inside as the cries of the beasts grew louder and ever nearer. The mice heard the terrible swishing of some great force through the dry grass, approaching like a crackling fire. After all were safely packed within the dark and damp-smelling log, Edmund ushered them off to one end away from the opening. The screams and movement on the outside grew louder and louder, till the very shadow of the beasts blanketed the log in blackness. Then—there was silence.

No noise. No movement. Just icy stillness.

And time. Endless, vacant. Fearful moments piling up one on top of another.

The mice stood in a huddled mass, exhausted and out of breath.

"Are they gone?" a tiny voice whispered in the stuffy darkness. "I'm frightened."

"Shhh!" Gabriel cautioned. "Not another word. Just listen!"

So they concentrated and strained their ears for the slightest sound of anything prowling outside. The mice were terrified, stuffed uncomfortably in the log, and still the moments dragged by. Many closed their eyes and quivered in the darkness. Others teetered on the verge of panic, wanting to scream and bolt back into the field. A few simply stood in a daze.

After many more minutes of torturous silence, Gabriel wondered if the coast was clear. Perhaps they had outwitted the beasts and could continue their journey in peace. Their fears may have been unfounded after all. He wondered if he should peek out and have a look. He was their leader after all, and the others were probably expecting him to do something. Gabriel cautiously headed towards the opening.

Suddenly the log shook violently. The mice were tossed about mercilessly like ships on a stormy sea. The dusk was again filled with the wicked cries of the hideous beasts. They attacked the log, tearing away at the rotten wood with sharp claws and teeth. Their eyes gleamed with a sickening green glow. The mice squeaked in terror, bustling about, but knowing full well that to leave was to face instant death.

The rocking and shaking continued. Tiny bits of wood fell upon the mice like hailstones as the beasts scratched at the log. Soon the long nails of one of the creatures pierced through the top, razor-sharp as it continually cut through the surface, getting closer and closer to the mice. They scattered to either end of the log, trapped, intently listening to the surrounding storm of voices. Time slipped away. All of their labors had resulted in this miserable end.

All seemed lost.

CHAPTER TWELVE

The Final Stretch

Bits of rotten wood rained on the mice as they squeaked in terror, some pushing blindly, others tumbling helplessly about. Outside, the frenzied cries of the beasts tore through the dusky air as they rocked the hollow log. The tangle of weeds and grass holding it tightly in place were ripped away clump by clump.

For a few moments though, Gabriel was unaware of the commotion as he desperately tried to think of a way out of their predicament. He regretted leading his friends into danger and feared they had only a few moments before the beasts would destroy them all. Florence's high-pitched voice dragged Gabriel back to reality.

"One of the beasts is almost inside!" she shrieked. "I can see its claw breaking through the wood."

"We'll never get away now!" another cried. "They'll kill us all! We should have stayed home."

"It's over…" others whispered in despair.

But not everyone was ready to give up yet. "Back to the opening at the other end of the log!" Edmund ordered. "We'll have to run for it. That's our only chance!"

Gabriel and a few of the others agreed, but many of the mice in their state of terror felt that such a move would mean instant death. The undecided ones were in too much shock to know what to do or whom to trust.

"Better that some of us survive by fleeing, than all of us die cowering here!" Gabriel shouted as the top of the log continued to collapse. The bony leg of one beast had nearly dug through as the rocking and jolting persisted. "Now whoever wants to take a chance, follow Edmund and me!"

Gabriel quickly scanned the shadowy faces to see who was with him. He noticed Violet among the crowd and saw fear and dread in her eyes, yet sensed a determined spirit that still wanted to fight. His brief glance calmed her and Gabriel knew that Violet would follow him wherever he might lead.

"Let's go!" Edmund said.

Half mad with terror, the mice followed Gabriel and Edmund down the log towards the opening, bouncing and stumbling as a storm of wood chips and dirt specks twirled about them. But their final hope was crushed when one of the beasts tried to break through the main entrance at the other end. Their only escape route was blocked.

"No way out now!" Florence cried. "Those infernal beasts!"

"Help us, Gabriel," Violet softly pleaded. "Tell us what to do."

Gabriel would have given his life to save Violet and the others if he only knew how. He watched his friends desperately look at him and Edmund for advice, for hope, for *anything* to save them. But Gabriel didn't know what to do. The cries of the beasts grew louder and more vicious.

Suddenly, two mice in back of the group, Lewis and another named Jalin, raced towards the far end of the log. The pair had been whispering to each other as Gabriel spoke. Lewis briefly turned around and called to Gabriel.

"Wait where you are till the way is clear to go! Jalin and I have an idea," he said.

"Get back here!" Gabriel ordered.

But Lewis wouldn't listen. At once, he and Jalin squeaked as loudly as they could and scratched their claws against the far side of the log. Forty-nine mice at the other end watched in stunned silence. Surely the beasts would hear them and locate their position from outside. Then Gabriel understood what the two mice were trying to do and his heart sank.

A few more moments passed when the rocking of the log finally stopped. The flurry of rotten debris ceased falling upon the mice. The beast that had dug its claw into the log disappeared. A dreadful silence fell except for the continual squeaking and scratching from Lewis and Jalin. The other mice looked mystified at their behavior. Florence prepared to run over and tell them to stop making noise, but Gabriel reluctantly held her back with a commanding stare.

Then in a flash, the beasts started to attack the log again, only this time all six gathered at the far end, taunted by the cries from Lewis and Jalin. The rocking and shaking continued amid a hail of dusty wood flakes and soil. Lewis shot a brief glance Gabriel's way, his eyes urging Gabriel to take this final chance for escape. It was the only way and both mice knew it. Gabriel nodded firmly at Lewis and tried to smile, and then Lewis turned back to his task with renewed determination.

"Let's get out of here," Gabriel whispered. "Lewis and Jalin are keeping the beasts occupied, but I fear they'll hold out only for a few moments. We have to flee now. There won't be a second chance."

So with Edmund leading the way, the mice squeezed through the hole at the bottom of the log one by one. They headed for the willow tree nearby as darkness deepened and a scattering of white stars burned above.

"They won't survive!" Florence said to Gabriel before exiting the log. "We can't let them face the beasts alone."

"Lewis and Jalin are our only hope, Florence. Hurry now!" he said, trying to get her to leave.

"But we can't abandon them!"

Simon heard Florence and scurried over to her. "I'll stay with them, Florence. You leave with the others," he said as he helped Gabriel push her into the field.

Gabriel was shocked to hear such brave talk from Simon. He pulled him aside as the remaining mice continued to file out.

"Simon, you can't stay here. The beasts will get *you* for certain! Follow me now. We're the last two."

"No!" he snapped. "Go, Gabriel. The beasts will realize any moment now that we're gone."

"Simon, I won't—"

"Leave, Gabriel! Save the others."

Simon didn't give his friend a chance to reply for he ran to the end of the shaking log with Lewis and Jalin. He joined in their squeaking and scratching to distract the beasts as the six ravenous creatures tore at the log.

Gabriel, knowing the danger Simon was in, wanted to stay with him. But he also knew he couldn't abandon the other mice. He was their leader. Yet something else made him feel uneasy. He sensed that Simon had again lost his ability to reason and was under the spell of the beasts. Gabriel knew it would be useless to argue and so promptly left to catch up with the others. As he raced through the dusky grass towards the willow tree, Gabriel believed he would never see his friend again.

Edmund led the group to the base of the nearby willow. The stone wall of the estate lay only a short distance away due south. The mice paused for a brief rest just as Gabriel showed up.

"Where are the others?" Florence asked. "Lewis and Jalin. And Simon. When are they coming?"

Gabriel couldn't answer that question. He informed the others that Simon had remained behind to help distract the beasts. Even now the mice could hear the dreadful cries of the creatures as their relentless attack continued in the tangled shadows.

"Then there's still hope," said Edmund. "Follow me to the wall now! We've tarried here long enough."

So the forty-eight remaining mice left the base of the willow tree and raced for the wall surrounding the estate. As twilight slipped away and darkness deepened, a thousand stars spilled across the sky. The moon began to rise in the east, giving the mice a final boost of hope. They raced through the grass.

The silvery disk was just past full and cast its light over the field and upon the wall. The gray stones loomed ahead, growing larger and larger by the moment. The grass was cut short here, so there wasn't any place to hide during this last leg of the journey. But that didn't seem to matter now. The mice were so close to their new home. So close to freedom and safety. So close.

Then a mournful wail, thin and skeletal, flew across the field like a bitter breeze. Again the mice heard the sound they dreaded most—the cries of the beasts.

"They're headed our way!" Gabriel shouted. "Run as fast as you can!"

The beasts closed in, six ragged figures followed by six wavy shadows stretched by the moonlight. The creatures had finished their attack on the log, and realizing that the other mice had escaped, pursued them with the fury of a lightning storm.

As the mice made a final dash towards the wall, Gabriel kept them together, running along the edge of the group. Then he heard a noise of swishing grass behind him and turned to confront his pursuer. It was only Simon. Gabriel was shocked and elated to see him alive, then a cloud passed over his heart.

"Where are Lewis and Jalin?" he asked, slowing down.

"They didn't make it!" was all that Simon said as he charged by.

Gabriel tried to catch up, but Simon proved much too fast. In a short while though, he and all the other mice stood at the base of the stone wall. Some darted restlessly about in the short grass, feeling exposed to the world. Others cowered in fear, convinced the end was at hand. Several scratched and clawed at the stones, not knowing what else to do.

Edmund tried to calm their fears. "Be patient! We'll be safe in a moment."

"Safe?" Chester cried. "How? How are we to get over this giant wall? It's too high. Not enough time to climb it."

"We'll be dinner for the beasts for certain!" added Elmer. "They'll be here any moment."

It was only too true. The beasts tore through the field, screaming madly in the night. Their glowing green eyes appeared to float in the shadows near the willow tree. Now they rushed towards the stone wall, getting closer and closer by the second.

"After coming all this way, only to be trapped here to die!" Florence wailed. "Why did we do it?"

Gabriel looked at Edmund for advice. He had trusted their guide every step of the way, but now they appeared to be at a dead end. What did Edmund have in mind? How were they to get beyond the wall? Gabriel didn't want to give up, but what other options were left?

"Must we run again?" Violet asked, voicing the sentiments of many others.

"Steady," Edmund said calmly as the beasts bore down on them. "Please *trust* me."

Gabriel didn't know what Edmund was waiting for. Time had almost run out when he decided to give the order for everyone to run and save themselves from the slaughter. But in the next instant, a small stone near the bottom of the wall began to wobble and was pulled inside. The head of a large brown mouse poked through the opening.

"Well it's about time you all got here," he said. "Where's Edmund?"

"I'm here, Toby!" Edmund cried. "But no time to talk. Get inside so the others can follow. Terrible danger is upon us!"

Toby didn't need a second warning. He stepped back inside the wall and signaled for the others to follow. So one by one, each mouse shot through the hole in the wall, following Toby through a short dark tunnel as the cries of the beasts magnified in the night air.

Only about half of the mice had entered when the beasts were in striking distance. "We'll never all make it in time!" Edmund said. "We have to stall those horrible creatures!"

In a flash, Edmund ran towards the beasts, who had already locked him in their sights. Then he shifted direction to the east, hoping to draw them away from the wall. Gabriel understood what Edmund was up to and joined him in his diversionary tactic, feeling it would be the last thing he'd ever do.

"Stay close to me, Gabriel!" Edmund called. "When the last mouse is inside, we'll break for the entrance ourselves."

The pair zigzagged through the grass, scurrying around stray rocks and shrubs to buy a little time, successfully keeping the beasts away from their friends. But Gabriel and Edmund both knew that they couldn't keep this chase up for very long. They would tire out soon and the beasts would have them unless they got back to the wall in short order.

Then Edmund noticed that the last mouse had passed through the wall, and Toby was again outside, urging them to hurry back. So he and Gabriel made a break for the wall with the beasts fast on their tails.

"I'm nearly out of breath," Gabriel panted. "I don't think I can make it."

"Sure you will!" Edmund urged him on. "We're nearly there. See! That's the opening. You go inside first."

Gabriel saw the short path to safety but realized that it was too late for both of them to make it. If he went inside first, the beasts would surely pounce on Edmund. He was certain Edmund realized this too. Gabriel had had enough. First Lewis and Jalin had given their lives for him, and now Edmund was about to make the same sacrifice. He wouldn't have it. Gabriel decided that if Edmund didn't have a chance, he couldn't allow himself one either. He prepared to confront the fury of the beasts side by side with Edmund.

But weariness won out. Without an ounce of strength left in his body, and as the howls of the beasts exploded, Gabriel collapsed in the soft grass. Edmund, on the brink of exhaustion himself, stopped near his friend in a futile effort to help.

"Gabriel, you must get up!"

"It's too late, Edmund. Just too late..."

And it was. The beasts had slowed down and encircled the two mice in the growing moonlight, closing in upon them step by step. Their green eyes burned with liquid fire, and hot stale breath sickened the mice till they nearly fainted. The six beasts bared their bloody, drooling teeth, and Gabriel saw the proof that Lewis and Jalin had indeed been killed. Now it was his and Edmund's turn. The end had finally arrived. Gabriel took a last glance at the wall. A new home had been so close, he thought as he closed his eyes to await the deadly strike.

At that moment, seven screeching black shadows swiftly descended, flailing their sharp claws at the beasts. The six creatures howled in pain as knife-like scratches seared across their backs and heads. They jumped wildly in the air, ignoring the two mice as they tried to fight back their attackers.

"Slink back to your wicked woods, you mischievous wretches, before we scratch your eyes out!"

Gabriel chuckled to himself when he heard Orville's wonderful voice. For it was he, Wilbur and five of their friends who challenged the beasts in dramatic style and in the nick of time. Their flapping wings and frenzied mid-air stabs kept the beasts at bay.

"Now's our chance," Edmund whispered. "To the wall!"

Gabriel, who had regained a bit of his strength, got to his feet and followed Edmund to the wall as fast as his legs could carry him. Toby waited there for the two of them.

"I thought you were both goners," he said. "Luckily those blackbirds saved your necks. Now get inside, as if I need to say *that* twice!"

Gabriel and Edmund slipped safely inside the hole, with Toby following swiftly behind. He pushed the first stone back into place. Then with the help of several other mice waiting inside, they replaced the few remaining stones inside the base of the wall till the entrance to the outside world was securely sealed. All the mice were now safe within the estate grounds.

Orville, Wilbur and the other birds, seeing that the mice were now out of danger, soared high above the beasts and sailed over the stone wall.

"That'll teach you meddlesome pests to fool with us!" Orville scolded. "That was payback for Lily and her young. Don't think we forgot! Just try to come back again and we'll give you worse than a few bloody scratches!" he cried as the seven flew out of sight.

The beasts, burning with rage, barreled towards the stone wall and hurled themselves against the rocks but to no avail. They screeched and wailed throughout the night, vowing revenge. But as the moon disappeared in the west over the hours, their voices also faded. And when a gray and dewy dawn stretched over the field, not a trace of them remained.

CHAPTER THIRTEEN

A New Home

The mice milled about on the other side of the wall—some bewildered, others elated, and everyone quite exhausted. Their journey ended in fireworks-fashion and all were now secure from the terrors of the wild.

As the mice chattered away, Gabriel silently watched the moon sail over the rock wall like a silver ship upon an open sea. For a brief moment he felt at peace, as if nothing could ever harm them again. His friends were safe and that was all that mattered. He noticed Violet among the crowd. Her clover-green eyes soaked in the moonlight as she talked with Florence and Elmer. Gabriel felt unimaginable happiness right now, pleased that he had guided Violet to a safe haven where they might get to know each other better. He looked forward to the days ahead.

Then he remembered Lewis and Jalin, and the moonlight no longer seemed as warm and inviting. Gabriel couldn't help feeling responsible for their deaths and wondered if a new home was worth the sacrifice. But if the other mice found security and happiness within the borders of the estate, then maybe Lewis and Jalin's deaths wouldn't be in vain. The news would be a shock to the others when they learned what had happened to their two friends. Gabriel would have Simon tell the story shortly, after the others had a few more moments to enjoy the escape. With so much to think about, Gabriel's head was swimming.

As the celebration continued, everyone congratulated Toby several times over for his excellent timing in getting the hole in the wall opened. He had performed admirably when it counted most.

"Don't give me *all* the credit," he said, wiggling his long-whiskered nose, above which sat a pair of large iron-gray eyes. "I had a well-trained team along side me. We had the last stone partially moved out of the way so that I could observe the goings-on in the field. I saw you racing towards the wall and so we pulled the stone inside as fast as we could."

Edmund then explained how the mice living on the estate grounds had constructed the secret opening in the wall by prying away five small stones near the bottom. "The first stone was free and we easily pulled it out. The middle three came apart quickly too. The frost had heaved that portion of the wall enough to loosen them up," he said.

"It took us several weeks to scratch away the mortar surrounding the last stone," Toby added. "But it was worth the effort. Now we have a convenient passage into the outside world if we ever get the desire to leave."

"I thought you had everything you wanted *inside*?" Gabriel asked.

"And so we do," Edmund continued. "But occasionally one of us gets the urge to spend a day by the willow tree or run around the field to explore. Mostly though, the opening is used to bring other mice inside."

"Luckily for us," said Florence. "But tell me, Edmund, if you didn't have the passage in the wall, how would we have gotten in?"

"I'm afraid the only other way onto the property is around front through the main entrance," Edmund said, bobbing his tail. "There's a large metal gate blocking it, which sometimes opens and closes by itself. But we would have been able to crawl under it with no difficulty. *That's* not the problem."

"What exactly *is* the problem?" Elmer wanted to know. "I thought life here wasn't filled with unpleasant surprises." He and the others sensed that Edmund had left some crucial point out of his explanation, and so they received their first lesson in living at the estate.

Edmund assured them there was nothing to worry about. "You see, a large and ferocious dog is chained outside the main gate. If he ever saw one of us roaming in that area, he'd pounce on us for sure. That's why we avoid going outside the gate."

"How *terrifically wonderful!*" Florence said, followed by a disgusted sigh. "We leave one group of beasts to live next to another."

"Not to worry," Toby said calmly. "Major Grump is never allowed to run freely inside the grounds."

To the mice's great relief, they learned that the dog was either tied to a chain outside the main gate, or else kept inside a chicken wire pen surrounding a huge oak tree also outside the stone wall. Whenever the dog was taken into the main house, he was always attached to a leash. Major Grump seemed quite content with his lot in life.

"Enough chattering about dogs and stone walls," Orville called from the branch of a nearby bush. He, Wilbur and the other five blackbirds had been listening to the conversation.

"Come down and join us!" Gabriel said. "The seven of you are heroes. How did you arrive when we needed you most?"

The birds fluttered down and joined the crowd of squeaking mice. "My impeccably good timing, of course," boasted Orville. "You should know by now, Gabriel, that I have a knack for grand entrances. When I do something, I do it right or not at all."

Gabriel was delighted to see Orville again, happy to observe that he hadn't become any more modest since their last encounter.

"Of course, Wilbur and the others had *nothing* to do with our rescue," Edmund ribbed Orville.

"Certainly they did. Why, it was Wilbur who informed me of the exact time you mice were leaving the frog pond for here," Orville said.

Wilbur then explained their part in the whole affair. "You see, Orville and I are old friends. We've been flying above this field for as long as I can remember. I told him all about your traveling plans after I met with Greenback."

"Wilbur, why didn't you tell us you knew Orville when you were introduced to us at the frog pond?" asked Florence.

"You never asked. Besides, there were more important matters to discuss at the time," he replied. "After I left to fetch Edmund to be your guide and led him back to the pond, I flew off to see my friend Orville, just as he requested."

Gabriel looked askance at Orville. "You *asked* Wilbur to meet with you? Why?"

"Silly mouse! To find out exactly what you and your band of fifty were up to. I didn't have any fears that you could reach the estate— providing you encountered no dangers out of the ordinary. But I had a suspicion that those dreadful beasts might pose a problem or two." Orville flapped his black wings, gently reflecting the moonlight. "So after your journey commenced, Wilbur, our other friends and I circled high up in the sky keeping an eye on your progress. Just in case some unlooked for danger arose."

Florence walked up to the bird and wiggled her nose in appreciation. "I always knew you had a soft spot in your heart, Orville, even if you won't admit it," she said.

"Balderdash!" exclaimed Orville as he snapped up a bug from the ground. "Watching you from above was just something to do to— uh—keep busy on a dreary day."

Wilbur then mentioned how he and Orville had seen the mice trapped inside the hollow log. "The boys and I were about to swoop down and attack then, but we watched all of you start to make a run for it without being pursued. We thought it best to hold off so as not to draw attention to you."

At the mention of that terrifying incident, Gabriel turned to Simon and inquired what had happened to Lewis and Jalin. Several of the mice looked around, realizing that they had not returned. Some assumed the pair had stayed with Simon and made it back safely with him. Others admitted they had been so frightened inside the hollow log that they couldn't remember *anything* that had happened there.

"The three of you saved our lives by giving us extra time to escape," Chester said gratefully. "But where are Lewis and Jalin now?"

Simon appeared reluctant to answer. Finally he muttered a few sentences with his eyes focused on the ground. "We held out as best we could inside the log. Then the beasts... They broke through. It was awful. We ran. I… I managed to escape. Lewis and Jalin were—killed. I wasn't able to help them. I tried, but…"

All were deeply saddened upon hearing the news and the celebrating abruptly ended. Orville, Wilbur and the other blackbirds flew home while many of the mice stayed up late into the night and reminisced about Lewis, Jalin and Livingston. Simon, though, slipped off by himself. He needed to be alone.

"He's probably distressed because he wasn't able to save Lewis and Jalin," Florence said.

"Perhaps if we give him some time, he'll come to terms with what happened," suggested Violet.

Gabriel agreed that Simon shouldn't be bothered now, but he wasn't totally convinced that Simon was upset about the death of his friends. Though it pained him to think it, Gabriel wondered if Simon truly escaped from the beasts or had been merely allowed to leave instead. How could he possibly have gotten away and not Lewis and Jalin? Gabriel knew he would have to confront Simon about the truth eventually, but didn't look forward to the task.

The sun shone dazzling yellow the next day, warming the ground and sparkling brilliantly off the pond water. After getting a tour of the estate grounds from Edmund and Toby, each of the mice went off in search of a place to live. A few chose spots near the small garden pond filled with frogs, having grown accustomed to such surroundings after spending the time at Greenback's pond. Others lived in the blossoming gardens or among tree roots while the rest settled in the taller grasses of the back lawns.

By the end of the second full day, this new neighborhood had become home. The mice frolicked through the grass and flowers, raced around the stone well, and occasionally sneaked up to the main house to browse around that area too. Everyone knew well enough not to stray too close to the main gate and Major Grump, however. All in all, the mice enjoyed their surroundings immensely and not one of them voiced a single complaint.

CHAPTER FOURTEEN

Explorations

Sparkling mornings and lazy afternoons dissolved into cool starry nights as the mice grew accustomed to life on the estate. Lush lawns, fragrant gardens and towering trees provided ample opportunities to explore. A string of perfect days, coupled with an abundance of food and the thrill of new discoveries, made the mice believe they hadn't a care in the world. Best of all, there were no beasts to worry about. No one could have imagined a better place to live.

On a particularly fine day in late August, Gabriel, Chester and Elmer wandered along the back wall discussing the plight of their friends they had left behind in the field. Now that he had grown used to the place, Gabriel admitted he felt a little guilty about living in a secure environment while Old Thackery, Fred, Doris and the others had to contend with the beasts.

"It's not fair," he said with a trace of bitterness. "Maybe I should travel back and see if any others would like to return with me. I'm sure I could find the way with little difficulty."

"Don't be silly," Chester advised. "We only arrived here a few days ago. The beasts are probably still angry at our escape and might be prowling about in the shadows. Let's wait till springtime like you promised when some of the younger mice will be ready to make the journey."

"Maybe by then the beasts will have forgotten us too," Elmer added with hope in his voice. "Perhaps they'll leave the forest and seek new territory before winter. Let them bother someone else for a change."

Gabriel admitted that that would suit him fine, but he didn't harbor high expectations for such an outcome. "I'm afraid the beasts are here to stay. They or their kind *always* seem to be lurking around the next tree or over the nearest hill. Always…"

Chester and Elmer didn't have a counter argument, so the trio continued on in gloomy silence. They fed upon a patch of toad stools growing near the base of the wall and the tasty treat raised their spirits. In time, the three took to chasing each other around a large stone well nearby. Though it towered high above them, the rocks it had been built with provided enough ridges and footholds for them to easily scale it. Chester dared that they should all climb up, so feeling rather brave on a full stomach, the mice scurried to the top like miniature mountain climbers.

They poked their noses over the edge then crawled onto the thick slate rim. It measured less than a foot wide all the way around, and the well stretched five feet across. From this vantage point, the mice spotted a round wooden well cover lying on the ground close by, surrounded by tufts of tall grass. It had slowly rotted away over the seasons. The well had obviously not been used for many years.

Gabriel plucked up the courage to walk to the inside edge of the rim and look inside the well. Chester and Elmer cautiously followed.

"Careful now, Gabriel," squeaked Elmer. "If you tumble in, there's no *way* you're getting out—even if you did survive the fall, which is unlikely. See how smooth the inside stones were cut."

A cool draft rose out of the well as the three mice inched their noses over the edge. Down, down below in an inky darkness, they slowly grew aware of their own tiny reflections staring back at them from a thin pool of water on the bottom.

"Wow! That's way far down," Chester whispered in giddy amazement. "I'll bet if the tallest tree in the field climbed into this well it wouldn't be able to see over the top."

"I'll bet if *any* tree climbed into this well, we'd be too shocked to even care how tall it was!" Gabriel said with a smirk as Elmer burst into a fit of laughter.

Having satisfied their curiosity, the three mice soon descended the well into the grass again and scampered off, nibbling on a few wildflowers here and there before heading towards home. As they neared one of the rock gardens and were about to go their separate ways, Gabriel noticed Violet near a clump of forget-me-nots, resting in the shade beneath its canopy of sky-blue petals.

"I'll see you two later," Gabriel said hastily to his friends, his heart racing. Chester and Elmer sensed his fondness for Violet and left him on his own without uttering so much as a playful remark.

"Well hello, Gabriel," she said when hearing him approach, unable to hide her joy. "What mischief have you and the boys been up to this afternoon?"

"Nothing terribly exciting or out of the ordinary," Gabriel replied, joining Violet under the shade. "This is a perfect spot to rest on a warm day."

"I discovered it the other evening while foraging and thought what a lovely place to while away a lazy afternoon. Don't you agree?"

Gabriel, who had been lost in Violet's clover-green eyes, sputtered out an answer. "Yes, yes! I think so too."

"Maybe one day we could stroll here together and talk for a spell," Violet suggested. "We really haven't been able to do that, what with all the traveling to get here, and now everyone scurrying about looking for new living quarters."

"That would be a fine idea," Gabriel said, unable to hide a smile. "I'm so glad you joined us on the journey, by the way. I meant to tell you that earlier. Just—just wanted you to know."

Violet stepped out into the sunlight, her light brown fur shimmering with a hint of red. "There's something I wanted to tell you too, Gabriel," she said, not looking directly at him.

"Oh?"

"I just wanted to say that—Well, I thought you were very brave to…" Violet turned and faced him. "I think you did a *wonderful* job as our leader, Gabriel. We wouldn't have made it, or even begun the trip, without your constant encouragement and good sense. We're all very proud of you, most especially me."

"Uh, thanks, Violet," Gabriel responded bashfully, not knowing what else to say. Though his legs were wobbly and his heart aflutter, Gabriel also felt full of confidence as if the world was at his command. Violet seemed to bring out the best in him, and Gabriel was so glad he had met her.

"Well…" Violet said.

"Well…" echoed Gabriel, still at a loss for words. "May I walk you home? That is, if you're *going* home."

"I'm going to stop by and see Florence. She's made her new home near the rock garden and asked me to visit when I had a chance," Violet said. "But I think it would be fine and lovely if you accompanied me there, Gabriel."

And so he did. Gabriel and Violet chatted as they walked through tall blades of sweet smelling grass, and then forged a path among the cool shade of a sprawling bed of myrtle. By the time they reached the rock garden, they felt as if they had talked for hours. They got along splendidly and couldn't wait to see each other again soon. Gabriel said he would stop by the next day. Violet made him promise, which he eagerly did.

Upon leaving Violet at the rock garden, Gabriel wandered about, carefree and aimless. He felt as if he could fly on a breeze and was certain the day would only get better.

Then he saw Simon in the distance.

Simon stood beneath a clump of rose bushes, vigorously scratching his claws against their woody stems. Gabriel hadn't talked with Simon very much since they arrived at the estate, believing his friend needed time alone to deal with his feelings about the deaths of Lewis and Jalin. Though at times he appeared not to be bothered by the incident, Gabriel believed that Simon was terribly upset. What other way *could* he feel? Gabriel decided that now was a good time to talk with his friend.

"Hello, Simon. What's going on? Wonderful afternoon, isn't it?"

Simon continued scratching his claws against the rose stems, sharpening them while making a small pile of wood shavings. "I suppose," he said indifferently. "If you like nice weather…"

"The weather *is* spectacular. But that's not the best thing about today. I just finished talking with Violet," he said, eager to tell Simon about his new infatuation. "She's very nice, don't you think?"

Simon nodded without much enthusiasm. "I guess."

"I promised to stop by and see her tomorrow. Maybe the two of us will take a long stroll by the back wall," he said dreamily.

"Whatever… Have a good time." Simon went on sharpening his claws, ignoring Gabriel as if he weren't present.

Gabriel noticed the emptiness in Simon's eyes and watched him for a few moments. "You sound rather irritated, Simon," he finally said, no longer in the mood to talk about his relationship with Violet. "Is something bothering you that you'd like to discuss? I'd be happy to listen."

"No."

"Simon, if—"

"I said no! Can't you hear?" Simon glared spitefully at Gabriel and started to walk away, then turned around. "I think it was a mistake moving to this place, if you must know. I don't think I like it. I feel so confined here."

Gabriel couldn't understand Simon's dislike for the surroundings, believing they now had everything a mouse could desire. "How can you *not* be pleased, Simon? There's so much room to roam about and many of our closest friends are here. And no beasts!"

Simon flashed a bitter glance Gabriel's way, as if he were about to leap at him. But instantly his mood changed and he wandered in the direction of the main house. Gabriel followed.

"I just don't like it here. I can't explain it fully, but I crave the openness of the outside and the challenge of the wild," Simon said.

"I suppose you could always go back home," Gabriel suggested. "The field is wide open."

Simon sighed in disgust. "I don't want to go back there either! Those mice are content hiding in their homes and doing nothing more. Most of them are cowards. Why, they wouldn't even risk the journey here."

"Simon, that's not fair. Some of them—"

Simon stopped in his tracks. "And we're not much better off shut up behind a stone wall. We're prisoners! Lazy and timid. And I'll tell you again, I *don't* like it!"

Gabriel stared at him, flabbergasted. "I don't know what to say, Simon. You *can* leave, you know. Nobody is forcing you to stay here."

"Maybe I *should* leave."

"Well then maybe you *should*!" Gabriel snapped, instantly regretting his words. He could plainly see that Simon was agitated and miserable, ready to explode. His friend needed understanding at the moment or a comforting word, but Gabriel hadn't the slightest idea what to say. He was angry at Simon but felt sorry for him at the same time.

"Oh, you don't understand!" Simon grumbled, walking away at a brisk pace. "Just don't follow me, okay? I want to be alone."

Gabriel stood in stunned silence, his mouth agape and his thoughts in a jumble. He knew Simon wasn't ready to talk and wondered if he had done the right thing by confronting him. As he turned and walked away, Gabriel wondered if he had lost his friend for good. He couldn't bear to lose another one.

Simon turned around a moment later and watched Gabriel leave. For an instant his anger subsided and he suddenly wished he could talk to his friend about the old days together in the field. He recalled all the fabulous times that he, Gabriel and Livingston had spent running through the grass under sunny skies and along the stream with a spring breeze. Everything had been so simple then, so perfect. Simon missed those days terribly. Now everything was wrong. If only the beasts had never existed, he considered. If only he had never stumbled upon that claw print in the sand. If only…

A sharp, steady noise drifting down from near the house shook Simon out of his daydream. He guessed it was Major Grump barking for his lunch.

During his second day at the estate, Simon had inadvertently met the Major. While wandering along the driveway in front of the main house at dusk that day, Simon had gathered up his courage to scurry all the way to the main gate, even though he had been warned not to explore this part of the property. The still air wrapped the shadows in warm caresses. Not a soul was around.

Simon approached the gate, two doors constructed of vertical metal bars spaced close enough so that only a mouse or a chipmunk could squeeze through. Deeming it safe enough, Simon decided to scoot under the gate to catch a peek of the outside. But he had hardly poked his nose through when a large brown and white dog leaped at the gate and took a swipe at Simon with its enormous paw. Simon pulled himself backwards to safety just in time as Major Grump, attached to a thin chain, jumped hysterically at the gate, barking up a storm.

Simon ran off to a patch of high grass nearby, quite shaken after his encounter with the Major. His heart pounded as the dog's bark still echoed in his ears. But something compelled him to take a second look, so he hurried back to the gate, making sure to stay behind it this time. The power of the dog fascinated him.

A moment later, one of the residents living in the main house, an older man, walked down the driveway and slipped outside the gate. He greeted Major Grump with a reprimand to be quiet. Simon watched as the man unhooked the dog from its chain and led Major Grump to a chicken wire pen nearby. The pen surrounded a large oak tree just outside the main wall, its branches sailing high into the sky and sprawling over the stone wall and above one of the lower rooftops of the house. Under the shade of the giant oak sat the Major's doghouse.

The man turned a small latch on the pen's gate and let Major Grump run inside his secured quarters, then closed the gate, relatched it and walked back up the driveway. The tall man closed the main gate behind him and retreated inside, shutting out the night.

Simon recalled that evening, considering himself lucky to have escaped the swipe of Major Grump's paw. Very lucky indeed. But since that first encounter with the dog, Simon somehow felt attracted to the main driveway gate and enjoyed the challenge of sneaking up on Major Grump and watching him from a safe distance.

Simon decided to visit the Major again this afternoon. He couldn't go back to Gabriel just now, not after the way he had treated him. Simon realized he didn't really want to talk to Gabriel anyhow. These dull and dreary surroundings depressed him, and Simon would rather observe Major Grump at the moment than talk to another mouse. Whether the Major was napping, eating or wildly jumping at a passing butterfly, the dog seemed more intriguing to Simon than any of his friends. He felt more akin to the huge slobbering dog right now than to Gabriel and the others. Simon considered for an instant if he felt the same way about the beasts too, but quickly shook that notion from his mind.

CHAPTER FIFTEEN

The Wall

A rush of warm air carried the scent of sweet corn from a nearby farm. Stars glistened ice-white against a black velvet sky as a band of crickets chirped merrily in the tall grass skirting the stone wall. Another glorious night had blossomed at the estate.

Ever since Long Legs had first described this place, many of the mice who had made the journey felt an instant bond to the frogs living here. They congregated around the garden pond from time to time or chose to live nearby. The mice were invited to visit as often as they liked.

It had been almost two weeks since the new residents settled in, and on this night many of the mice gathered late at the pond to talk with the frogs and share stories. Gabriel and Simon were selected as the main storytellers since they had been the first mice to meet Greenback at the pond in the field. Gabriel was honored to relate the tale of their travels, and was particularly delighted when Simon agreed to join the festivities. Simon acted less distant and moody since their run-in a few days ago. Gabriel believed Simon had experienced a change of heart and hoped this marked the end of his strange behavior that had begun after their first trip to the woods in search of the beasts.

The frogs craved details about the other pond. Since many relatives and friends lived there, they wanted an update on their long lost companions. So as the mice lounged among the cattails and tall grasses on the water's edge and the frogs bobbed gently on their lily pads, Gabriel and Simon unfolded their adventurous tale long into the night. The frogs croaked in appreciation at the stories, asking many questions along the way.

"...and *that's* how we made it over the creek—one stone at a time!" Gabriel later continued to his spellbound audience, enjoying his role as storyteller. "Not much happened after that until we reached the hollow log just beyond a huge rock lying in the field."

"This is an *exciting* part coming up!" Elmer exclaimed.

Then, in chilling detail, Gabriel described the cries of the beasts sailing through the twilight air and how the mice had to make a run for their lives. When he reached the point in the story where the beasts had trapped them in the hollow log, his exuberance waned. He paused uneasily, wanting to forget the incident. Gabriel feared that mentioning the attack, and Lewis and Jalin's brave last stand, might upset Simon and cause him to lapse into his old behavior. He didn't want to take that chance.

"Perhaps we should finish this another time," Gabriel said. "I *have* been rambling on. You frogs must be bored to tears."

"Of course they're not!" Florence said. "I'm still interested and I already *know* what happened."

"Talk on! Talk on!" a frog named Widefoot interjected. "I haven't heard such a riveting tale since I was a tadpole."

"You are quite an excellent storyteller," a second frog said. His name was Leaper. "You're a first-rate spinner of tales."

"Here, here!" Toby agreed, his large eyes bubbling with anticipation. His tail swayed like a willow branch in the wind as he eagerly awaited every detail.

"Certainly you didn't *forget* what happened next, did you?" Florence added. "Shall I finish the story myself?"

"No!" Gabriel hastily answered.

"Then I *will!*" Simon jumped in. "Our friends are patiently waiting to hear the conclusion, and besides, Gabriel, you've been talking too long. It's my turn."

The frogs, assembled like spectators in a king's court, croaked in agreement. Dozens of green shiny bodies gleamed in the starlight.

"Here's what happened next," Simon continued. "You see, we ran and hid inside this rotten hollow log to escape the beasts. They had secretly followed us to the estate, pursuing us with the fury of a brush fire. Now we were trapped. So then we…"

As Simon told the story, Gabriel listened in amazement that his friend could talk about the vicious beasts and not be overcome by their very mention. Surely Simon must be cured now, Gabriel hoped. He wished it so with his whole heart, wanting his friend to return to his old self. Gabriel listened, mesmerized as Simon's words carried them through the night.

After the story was finished, and the frogs grew tired of requesting repeats of their favorite parts, they one by one slipped into the water or hid among the cattails for the night, leaving the mice alone. Several of the mice then scurried off to their holes to catch some sleep while others disappeared into the darkness for a late night meal. Dawn still lay many hours away as thin wisps of frosty clouds drifted lazily through the sky and the warm winds took on a pre-autumn chill.

Gabriel curled up at the base of a towering cattail for a quick nap, but awoke a few hours later, thinking for a moment that he was back in his hole. All was quiet as the cool of the night reached deep into his bones. The frogs and the other mice were nowhere in sight, so Gabriel decided to take a short walk around the grounds to warm up. Perhaps then he'd search for a quick bite to eat.

A silvery blanket of dew coated the grass and Gabriel stopped now and then to lick the cool droplets off the blades. He happened upon a pine cone that dropped from a nearby tree and gnawed at its pointy scales to amuse himself. At last Gabriel neared the well. He wondered if he were brave enough to climb to the top alone this time and in the dark no less, then had the sudden urge to do so. Gabriel hoped such a daring act would impress Violet when he told her about it.

Putting aside any fears, he found a secure footing at the base of the well and scaled the stony obstacle. The rocks were wet from the night air and once or twice Gabriel nearly lost his footing. But he scratched his way up and up and was only slightly out of breath when emerging onto the slate rim.

Gabriel rested a moment and then walked cautiously around the smooth sleek surface along the outside edge. He picked up his pace and soon found the courage to scramble swiftly around the well. The wind felt crisp against his face and whiskers as his tiny claws scratched rhythmically over the shiny slate. At one point Gabriel nearly slipped off into the grass, so he stopped to rest again, sitting on his hind legs and glancing up at the stars. A slender crescent moon, as thin and delicate as a spider's webbing, peeked over the eastern horizon.

After a moment, Gabriel decided to act a little bit braver and take a peek over the inside edge of the well. The task seemed more daunting in the black of night than when he had chanced it with Chester and Elmer a few days before. Without hesitation, Gabriel crept across the rim till his nose poked over the side. Again he could feel a cool draft rise up from the depths, but the utter blackness within proved unsettling. After several moments had passed, Gabriel could barely discern the few inches of inky rainwater resting on the bottom. He was amazed to see his tiny reflection silhouetted in the watery mirror so far below.

Gabriel decided he had had enough excitement for one night and prepared to go home and back to sleep. As he was about to begin his descent from the well, he thought he heard a sound in the distance. Gabriel pricked up his ears and listened carefully across the cool pre-dawn air. Silence. Had his imagination gotten the best of him? But there it was again—a sound not altogether pleasant and too close for his liking. For a moment, Gabriel believed he heard the subtle chanting of the word *remember*.

He stood on his hind legs and surveyed the area, again listening attentively. Gabriel was certain beyond a doubt that he heard *something*. A chant? A whisper? Some low discordant sound filled the air. And what was that now in the mix? Perhaps laughter of an unpleasant sort? Or a hiss? Gabriel knew he must investigate at once.

He scurried down the well and ran towards the source of the noise. Gabriel slowly edged his way to the estate wall near the secret opening and realized that the strange sounds seemed to emanate from the other side of the wall. He listened again to make sure, and then all was silent. Gabriel didn't know what to think.

He ran up and down the line of the wall in the thickening gray light, but discovered nothing and heard no further sounds. Ready to give up, Gabriel noticed a small shape moving in the grass up ahead. It moved away from him so Gabriel trailed cautiously. Then he sighed with relief.

"Simon! What are you doing here? Trying to scare me, no doubt. Well your little joke wasn't the least bit amusing," Gabriel said playfully.

Simon didn't respond and continued walking slowly and deliberately forward. Gabriel scrambled to catch up with his friend, scolding him for making all those dreadful noises earlier. But Simon neither answered nor turned around to look at Gabriel. He only kept walking.

"Simon, I'm talking to you."

No reply.

Gabriel's slight indignation transformed into suspicion. Simon appeared to be asleep, yet his eyes were wide open as he plodded through the grass without stumbling over any stones or twigs in his way. Gabriel followed Simon to his hole beneath some shrubbery roots and watched him go inside.

Gabriel remained outside for several minutes and scratched his head, hoping Simon might pop back out. But he never did as the stars faded and the sky slowly grew a whitish-gray. Gabriel couldn't fathom what had happened to his friend. The good times the two had shared at the garden pond during the night melted before Gabriel's eyes. Once again he feared that Simon was not himself, and that somehow his fascination with the beasts was making him act erratically. Gabriel didn't know how to help him. Perhaps he never could.

CHAPTER SIXTEEN

Lights, Tents, Tables and Chairs

After an uneventful week had passed, something happened that threw the community of mice into a state of frenzied anticipation. One warm afternoon, several men dressed in dark blue coveralls and yellow caps emerged from three white vans that had rolled up the driveway, passed through the main gate and parked on the estate grounds. The men quickly opened the back doors of the vehicles, removed several objects of various shapes and sizes, then spread over the lawn like an army of ants and went to work.

The men first pitched three large canvas canopies, each decorated with wide green and white stripes. They pounded wooden stakes into the ground and fastened ropes to them to secure the metal frame poles. Next they pulled long rectangular tables out of the van and set them up all over the grounds—some under the canopies and others beneath shade trees. A few of the workers covered the tables with long sheets of shiny white paper while others set up dozens of metal folding chairs. And everywhere, strings of tiny colored lights were draped and twisted in record speed—along the canopy ropes and across the eaves of the house, and over bushes and around the trunks and branches of smaller trees. Some even entwined the iron rails of the main driveway gate. It seemed as if a summer beach carnival and Christmas had arrived simultaneously.

"What in the wide world is happening, Toby?" asked Gabriel as he viewed the spectacle from a safe distance behind a tuft of clover. "I've never seen anything like it. People are crawling all over the place. Is this an invasion?"

"Relax," Toby said, chuckling at Gabriel's jittery apprehension. "We have nothing to worry about. This happens every year during the waning days of summer."

"It does?"

"As certain as autumn follows. I'm surprised Edmund didn't mention this to you on your travels."

Gabriel scratched behind his ear. "I *do* recall him saying that you mice tended to keep away from the human activity most of the time *except* near one particular day. But I didn't give it much thought because I was too concerned about getting my friends safely to the estate."

"Well that particular day is almost here," Toby said. "I know for certain because of all this activity." He peered excitedly through the clover stems at the commotion, then retreated into the shadowy tuft and spoke softly to Gabriel. "For two days these strangely dressed men decorate the estate with lights, tents, tables and chairs. Tomorrow they'll bring in fresh bundles of fragrant flowers and hang up beautiful ornaments. But that's not the best part, Gabriel."

"No? Then what is the best part, Toby?"

"The *big day*!" he said in dramatic fashion, his wide eyes ready to pop. "The day we mice look forward to all year. You were lucky enough to arrive just in time to celebrate with us."

Gabriel couldn't contain his excitement. Nothing had ever happened in the field to compare to this. "When is the big day, and what's so special about it?"

"*When* it is, is soon. Usually the day after these men leave for good. What's so *special* about it is—well, that's nearly indescribable," Toby said, dreamily contemplating the big day. "But I'll try."

"Please do!"

"First, several people in the house dressed in fancy attire parade outside carrying huge platters and bowls of the most delicious tasting food you could ever imagine."

"Really?"

"That's the absolute truth, Gabriel. Cold fruits piled high or cut into fancy shapes. Strawberries and blackberries, watermelon and grapes. Others I've never even seen before. Then there are plates of various meats, sliced or rolled up. And some are cut into little chunks with cheeses and vegetables, all pressed between colorful crackers. And to top it off, the sweetest tasting dishes not found anywhere in the wild!" Toby squeaked. "Creamy and crumbly and decorated with fancy swirls and flowers."

"But who is all the celebrating for?" Gabriel desperately wanted to know. He found it difficult to imagine who could be so exalted as to receive such an extraordinary banquet. Toby clarified the situation.

"The celebrating isn't to honor one person, Gabriel. It's for everybody! After all the food has been set out, and the lights and music are alive, a vast horde of people arrive at the estate in their noisy metal machines. They're dressed in splendid clothes too. They eat and drink and talk and laugh and listen to the music. They usually begin at mid-afternoon, and many don't leave until the next day!"

Gabriel thought himself the luckiest mouse in the world. What a treat it would be to witness such a gala. He only wished the party were that very night.

"But that's not the best part," Toby added.

"You mean there's *more*?" Gabriel asked, his mouth agape, trying to figure out how the spectacle could possibly get any better.

"Oh, yes! Much more. You see, shortly after sunset, a beautifully dressed lady emerges from the main house and rings a large brass bell. When hearing that, the music stops and all the people head inside for the rest of the evening. And guess what they do next, Gabriel?"

"Tell me at once!" Gabriel said, nibbling on the clover.

"They all sit down at large tables to gobble up an even *bigger* feast than they had outdoors!"

"I can't believe a word of it, Toby," Gabriel said, wiggling his nose. "Your story gets more incredible with each word you speak."

"I'm telling you the absolute truth!"

"How can you know what goes on inside the main house?" he asked, clutching a sprig of clover while listening.

"Well, two summers ago, one of the mice had the courage to sneak inside. When he returned, he described all the food that had been prepared. Tables filled with even more treats than those outdoors. And there were burning sticks of wax up and down the centers, and everyone drank lovely colored drinks out of glass holders. He would have seen more but was chased away by a screaming little girl with a broom."

Gabriel sighed. "That must have been a wonderful sight to behold. What a lucky mouse. But what happens after all the people go inside? Does that mean we don't ever see them again, Toby?"

"You'll see them when they leave in their riding machines, of course. Most likely the next day."

"That's too bad," Gabriel sadly said. "I would like to watch them merrymaking all night long. But I suppose I should be contented that they stay outside in the daytime."

Toby looked at Gabriel dumbfounded, his face bunched up in a sour wrinkle. Then he burst out laughing. "Why you silly little mouse! Aren't you thinking this morning? Is the hot sun melting your commonsense? It's that moment when all the people finally go *inside* that we mice wait for!"

"What do you mean?"

"Once the people are out of the way, then all of us can indulge in a feast of our own. You'll be astounded at the food those creatures drop to the ground and on the lawn furniture. I ate so much last year that I nearly burst. And *still* I was able to store away enough food to last until the middle of autumn," Toby said proudly. "Those people are fun to watch, but I like it better when they go indoors. Gabriel, you'll have the time of your life!"

A feast. Gabriel had never experienced anything like it in the wild or had even imagined such an event. How fortunate he had arrived at the estate when he did.

Just then Gabriel and Toby had to quickly abandon their spot in the clover as one of the men in the dark blue coveralls fast approached. He pushed a noisy contraption that tore up the grass and spit it to one side. The mice, not wanting to end up like the shredded grass, retreated to their homes to discuss the upcoming festivities with the others.

Violet and Florence leaped in the air when Gabriel broke the news. Simon seemed nearly as ecstatic later that afternoon when Gabriel told him about the big day. That pleased Gabriel very much. He felt encouraged that Simon took an interest in the news. Though he had appeared to be in especially good spirits over the last week, Gabriel still worried that something was not right with his friend.

Gabriel recalled hearing those strange noises last week by the well. The image of Simon walking trance-like back to his hole late at night still haunted him. Gabriel never could explain the situation or confronted Simon about it. He grew doubly worried when he caught Simon near the wall only two nights later in the same transfixed state. The strange noises had again permeated the air. Gabriel tried several times to ask Simon about what was going on, but always backed down at the last moment. He feared Simon might lose his temper again and reverse any progress he seemed to be making in his recovery. Gabriel decided to keep a close but secret watch on his friend's activities.

But in anticipation of the upcoming party, Gabriel let his suspicions rest for the time being. After the lawns had been mowed, Gabriel walked with Simon back towards the main house to watch the workers' progress in setting up for the festivities. Gabriel thought that spending time with Simon rather than questioning him repeatedly might do his friend more good.

"Even Major Grump will be lucky enough to see some of the goings-on," Gabriel joked. "The men even strung lights along the main gate. The Major should like that, though I'd venture to guess that he'll be kept in his pen that day. He'd probably jump on the guests otherwise."

"Most likely," Simon agreed as he watched the men diligently perform their tasks.

A few gray clouds soon drifted overhead, blotting out the sun. With late-afternoon shadows in abundance, the men decided to turn on the lights to test them. In a few moments, hundreds of tiny glass lights blinked on like stars. Only a few bulbs needed to be replaced.

111

As Gabriel looked on in wonder, Simon noticed that all the lights strung along the main gate were in working order. He gazed at them intently, unblinking. The green lights particularly captured his attention. Simon heard Major Grump barking in the driveway like some distant voice in a dream. He studied the green lights and listened steadfastly to the sharp barks, allowing nothing else to tear his attention away.

CHAPTER SEVENTEEN

The Trouble With Simon

"What a glorious morning!" Violet exclaimed as she and Gabriel foraged in the early morning sun. The air held a bracing chill and the grass glistened with drops of frosty dew. The pair scampered through the wet blades beyond the rock garden, nuzzling noses and squeaking with delight, only pausing now and then to let the rising sun warm their backs.

"It *is* a wonderful day, Violet, especially since I'm here with you," Gabriel replied. "Will you accompany me to the feast tomorrow? We'll have a terrific time."

"Of course I will, Gabriel. There's no one else I'd rather go with," Violet said.

The mice had talked about nothing else since yesterday. The big day, as Toby had named it, was a momentous event that no one wanted to miss. Gabriel only wished that his friends back home in the field could join them at the party.

"By the way, how's Simon feeling this morning?" Violet asked. "He's been rather cheerful lately. I do hope he snapped out of his doldrums for good."

113

"I haven't seen Simon," Gabriel said as he stood on his hind legs and inhaled a draft of cool morning air. "He might be searching for food with Chester or Elmer."

"I saw those two shortly before I caught up with you," she replied. "Simon wasn't with them. I wonder if he's even awake yet. Simon *does* sleep a lot lately, even more than Livingston used to. Maybe we should invite him to come along with us to the feast tomorrow night," Violet suggested. "To keep up his spirits."

"Uh, good idea," Gabriel said, somewhat distracted. Violet's remark about Simon sleeping too much made him reconsider an earlier decision. "Would you excuse me for a few moments, Violet? I think I should check on Simon right now. There's something I've wanted to ask him, but kept putting off. I don't think I should any longer."

"All right," Violet said, a bit concerned. "Is everything okay, Gabriel? You seem ill at ease all of a sudden."

"A little bit. But I'll explain later, Violet. I really need to talk to Simon now."

"Good luck then. I'll see you later."

"Okay," Gabriel said, flashing a quick smile. Then he bounded off, following a lengthy stretch of morning shadows cast over lush green lawns.

Gabriel hurried to Simon's hole beneath some shrubbery roots and peeked inside. Sure enough, there in his dark quarters lay Simon, curled up atop a pile of grass clippings and shredded leaves, fast asleep. Gabriel wrinkled his nose then nudged Simon, squeaking directly into his ear.

"Wake up, lazy mouse! It's nearly mid-morning. Don't think you can sleep away the entire day."

Simon stirred and slowly opened an eye, staring grumpily at Gabriel. He yawned and scratched behind an ear before getting to his feet. "Why—why are you here, Gabriel? Something the matter?"

"Just wondering why you aren't out and about. Thought you might have fallen into the well," Gabriel said, trying to make a joke. But inside he felt very concerned for his friend and couldn't hide his true feelings any longer. "You *have* been sleeping quite a lot these past few days, Simon. Why so tired?"

"That's no concern of yours!" he snapped. Simon was still half asleep and didn't mean to yell at Gabriel. "Leave me alone for a while longer. I'll—I'll join you later for a bite to eat."

"I've already eaten, but that's not important." Gabriel locked gazes with Simon, like a parent confronting a disobedient child. "There's something else that's been bothering me. I meant to talk to you about it on several occasions, Simon, but... Well, I didn't think I should ask you at first because..."

"What *are* you babbling about?" Simon muttered, rubbing his eyes. A few delicate rays of sun slipped inside, dispelling some of the darkness.

"It's just that...um..."

"Please say whatever you have to say quickly, and then leave me alone."

"I will." Gabriel let out a sharp breath between his teeth then glared at Simon. "Were you out by the wall again last night listening to those strange voices?"

"What? What are you talking about?"

"Now don't try to deny it."

"And why did you say *again*? Have you been following me?"

"I was concerned about you. I saw you there very late two nights ago, and another time several days before that when I happened to be near the well." Gabriel explained how he had heard strange noises and saw Simon walk in a trance-like state from the wall to his hole. "You looked like you were walking in your sleep."

"That's ridiculous, Gabriel. Why are you making up such stories? I didn't do any of that," said Simon defensively. "I think I'd remember if I did. Now if you're finished telling these tall tales, please leave, Gabriel, so I can rest for a while longer. I really want to be left alone!"

Gabriel prepared to argue the point, not wanting the situation to fester. But he saw how tired and dejected Simon appeared and felt sorry for him. Gabriel believed that maybe Simon really couldn't recall his nighttime walks to the wall. He was no closer to the truth about why his friend behaved so strangely after dark. He left Simon so he could get some more sleep.

As the hours slipped by, Gabriel tried not to think about Simon's problem. Instead, he concentrated on the men in the dark blue coveralls as they completed the final touches for the next day's festivities. He, Chester and Elmer hid by a rose bush near one of the canopies that afternoon and watched the men hang additional decorations, distribute bunches of flowers and rearrange tables and chairs according to the last-minute wishes of a lady from the main house. Gabriel wanted to bring Simon along but hadn't seen a trace of him since morning. A young sparrow living in a nearby tree finally provided the answer to his whereabouts.

"So you've seen our friend?" Gabriel inquired as he, Chester and Elmer headed home a short while later.

"He's fine," the sparrow said, pecking at the ground for something to eat. "I saw him near the main gate as I flew over."

"What's Simon doing there?" Elmer wondered. "He's taking a risk with Major Grump just on the other side."

"He's in no apparent danger," the sparrow continued. "That strange mouse just sits hidden in some grass near the gate and gazes outside the estate. He's been there today since the sun climbed high in the sky. The only reason I took notice is because he's been stationed there every afternoon for the past seven days."

"Seven days?"

The sparrow nodded. "I fly over that area at least a dozen times each day, and I have excellent eyesight. Why, I've spotted your friend planted there like a rock for hours at a time. Doesn't he have anything better to do? Strange behavior if you ask me," the sparrow said before snapping up an ant. "But then again, he *is* a mouse."

"Thanks very much for the information," Gabriel said. "I'm glad to know Simon isn't in any trouble."

"Happy to be of service," the sparrow replied. "Now there's work to be done." With that, he flew out of sight.

"What an odd bit of news, don't you think?" Chester asked.

"I don't know what's gotten into Simon," said Elmer. "Ever since we arrived here, he's been sort of, well… Standoffish?"

"Distant," Chester added.

"Aloof!" Elmer exclaimed.

"All of the above," Gabriel said quietly.

Chester and Elmer wanted to go to the main gate that very moment and confront Simon about his peculiar behavior. As much as he wanted to go along too, Gabriel advised against it.

"Some strange things are going on with Simon that I'm unable to explain yet. Be patient. Let's give him time to return home," Gabriel said. "I have a feeling he'll come back to his hole before nightfall and probably won't talk to a soul the rest of the day."

Gabriel's hunch proved correct. Simon returned to his hole beneath the shrubbery and went directly to sleep while the sun still hung over the western horizon. After leaving Chester and Elmer, Gabriel decided to solve this mystery once and for all. He staked out a hiding spot in some grass near Simon's hole and waited for darkness, determined to find out exactly what Simon had been up to these last several nights.

And so he waited, and waited and waited…

Gabriel opened his eyes to darkness. An icy chill gripped the air and the stars had clouded over. He poked his nose through the grass to get his bearings, realizing he had fallen asleep on the watch. Where was Simon?

Gabriel raced to Simon's hole and peeked inside. Empty. He was too late.

"To the wall!" Gabriel said to himself. "Simon must be there."

Gabriel ran through the cool grass, past the well and towards the stone wall when he heard the sounds. Just like the last time. A low steady chanting, mixed with hisses and laughter, emanated from the other side of the wall. The sounds disturbed him like an uneasy dream. What Gabriel saw next truly astounded him.

The secret passage at the base of the wall had been opened. Five stones lay scattered on the ground in the pale light of the sinking first quarter moon. The noises on the other side grew louder and more sinister. Again, Gabriel thought he heard the word *remember* being chanted, and then all was quiet. He wanted to look through the opening but grew afraid. An instant later he was flabbergasted when he saw Simon emerge through the passage back onto the estate grounds.

"What *is* he doing?" Gabriel whispered.

Slowly and carefully, Simon pushed each of the five stones and replaced them one by one into the wall with ease. The same task had taken Toby much longer, though he was a larger mouse and even had some help. Gabriel wondered how Simon possessed such strength.

After blocking up the wall securely, Simon walked back to his hole in a trance-like state. He walked past Gabriel but didn't notice him or utter a word. Gabriel looked on in disbelief, awash in frustration and concern.

Then the noises behind the wall sounded again, startling him. Gabriel listened for a few moments, annoyed by the hissing and laughter and its power over Simon. But slowly the sounds took on a rather pleasant tone, and Gabriel thought they were calling his name.

"Who's there?" he cried out, ignoring Simon for the moment. He walked over towards the blocked passageway. "Tell me who's there?"

Gabriel was never quite sure of the words uttered in reply, but they sounded soothing to the ear. Very pleasant and comforting in the dark of night. He thought he heard his name floating on the late summer air. Gabriel listened for several moments, thinking that it might be a good idea to meet whoever was calling him.

"I'm here…" he whispered, looking up at the wall, gazing fixedly at the top stones. He would never be able to climb that height. There was only one way to get through and meet his new friends. Gabriel reached for the first stone blocking the secret passage and prepared to remove it.

At that moment on the other side of the estate, Major Grump barked from inside his pen, startling Gabriel. He woke from his stupor and quickly stepped back from the wall. He could still hear the voices, but they again sounded bitter and thin. Gabriel now realized with horror that the beasts waited on the other side of the wall and nearly had him under their spell. He shuddered and raced madly towards home.

CHAPTER EIGHTEEN

The Big Day

Gabriel went to see Simon early the next morning, expecting to find him in a deep sleep. Instead, he was very much awake in his tiny quarters, pacing frantically from wall to wall. Gabriel thought Simon looked as fidgety as a fish out of water and believed he might collapse from exhaustion at any moment. He slipped inside to surprise him.

"Good morning, Simon! I'm glad to see you're wide awake instead of lying about like a lump of wet dirt." Gabriel did his best to put on a cheerful air.

Simon spun around, startled by Gabriel's entrance. "What are you doing here?" he asked sharply, then suddenly calmed down and ceased his troubled pacing. "I mean, what brings you by so early?" he gently added.

Gabriel felt ill at ease with Simon's sudden shift in mood. It only convinced him even more that Simon was not well.

"I can't avoid the ugly truth any longer, Simon. I saw you outside again late last night. You were down by the wall behind the main house."

"That's ridiculous!" Simon protested. "I was here all night. I slept from dusk till dawn."

"I'll agree with you on that point," Gabriel said sadly. "You probably *did* sleep through the night, but you were definitely not curled up here in your hole. I saw you outside, but you didn't recognize me. Just like on those other occasions. You were in a kind of trance."

"I won't listen to this!"

"Can't you remember, Simon?"

Simon stared at Gabriel with wide pleading eyes. His sandy-colored fur appeared ashy gray in the faint light. He tried to laugh at Gabriel's story but only managed to shake his head in bewilderment.

"You're—you're making up this whole strange story to confuse me. I don't know why you're doing this, Gabriel, but I wish you'd stop. It's not funny!" Simon looked even more distressed now and paced the floor again, trying to avoid Gabriel's piercing gaze.

"You may not want to hear the truth, Simon, but you have to. I saw you by the wall last night near the secret entrance. I heard strange voices on the other side. I'm telling you the truth! You've got to believe me."

"No I don't. You're lying!"

Gabriel cringed with frustration. "Last night you went through the passage in the wall to the other side where the voices originated. I'm not lying. Why would I? I saw you return to our side with my own eyes."

"I didn't!"

"You *did*, Simon." Gabriel stood nose to nose with his friend. "I watched you block up the wall with stones, then head for home as if you were walking in your sleep."

"Impossible, Gabriel! Listen to me!"

"Listen to *me*!"

"No!"

"You met with the *beasts*, Simon! Admit it!" shouted Gabriel, relieved that he had finally spoken the awful truth. He looked at Simon with pity. "You met with the beasts," he softly repeated. "And you're under their spell."

At this, Simon squeaked as if he had been pricked by a thorn, and then lunged at Gabriel head first. The two rolled in the dirt, scratching and hissing, their tails flailing in the air. Simon tried to sink his teeth into Gabriel's shoulder, but Gabriel, not realizing his strength, threw Simon off and sent him sailing to the far end of the hole where he lay whimpering on the cold ground.

Gabriel's heart pounded as he caught his breath, all the while keeping a close eye on Simon. He cautiously walked over to him, realizing that all the fight had gone out of his friend. "Are you all right?" he asked gruffly. "Did I hurt you?"

Simon looked up with anguished eyes, no longer plagued with anger or bitterness. A tiny drop of blood ran down his left leg where Gabriel had scratched him. He licked his wound. "I—I'm sorry, Gabriel. I don't know what came over me," he said after he finished tending his injury. "I don't know what's the matter with me. I feel…"

Gabriel sighed as Simon got to his feet. "It's the beasts, Simon. *They* are what's the matter with you. How long have you been seeing them?"

"I *haven't* been seeing them!" Simon cried, though not believing his own words. "At least I don't think so." He held the end of his tail, appearing frail and scared. "I'll admit I've had strange dreams about the beasts lately. In them, I would go to the wall and hear voices on the other side. Ugly sounding voices, but sweet and alluring at the same time. I can't explain it. Then somehow I would get the strength to remove the stones and meet with the beasts waiting in the field. They would talk to me and tell me things to remember, and slowly I would begin to feel like them. I didn't want to leave, but they always made me return home."

"What did they tell you?" Gabriel gently asked. "What did they tell you to remember?"

"I—I don't know. I can't recall. Isn't that strange? But then it doesn't really matter because it was only a dream, right?" Simon fearfully whispered those words as he looked helplessly at Gabriel. "At least I hoped it was. But if you say you saw me at the wall, then I guess I wasn't dreaming after all." Simon shuddered and covered his eyes. "Do the beasts own me, Gabriel?"

Gabriel didn't know what to say. He had finally pried the truth from Simon, but now he didn't know how to deal with it. What an awful situation, he thought, wondering how such a thing could have happened. Gabriel recalled the wild storm that had raged weeks ago, though it seemed years. With a flash of lightning, the beasts were driven from their barn and set loose upon the field across the road. But even now, though secure behind the stone wall of the estate, the mice were still pursued and haunted by the enemy.

"The beasts don't own you," Gabriel finally replied, trying to believe his own words. "But they *are* influencing you. You must be strong and resist them. Don't ever go back to the wall at night. *Ever!* If you never speak to them again, then they can't turn you to their will." Simon uncovered his eyes and looked up. "In time, maybe, you'll return to your old self."

"Maybe…" Simon whispered, crawling into a corner and keeping silent for several moments. "Gabriel, there's something else I need to tell you," he finally said amid the shadows. "I've kept it secret but I have to let somebody know."

"What is it?"

"Well, I—I have to tell you that…" Simon didn't know how to begin, so he plunged into the story. "Remember when we were trapped inside the hollow log?"

"Yes. You stayed behind with Lewis and Jalin. The three of you bought us precious time to escape."

Simon nodded dejectedly. "Yes, but… I didn't stay out of loyalty to my friends, or because I was so brave. I stayed with Lewis and Jalin because—"

"Yes, Simon?"

"Because—because I sensed the beasts had *commanded* me to stay. I really didn't want to, but somehow they made me. I felt I didn't have a choice."

A chill ran through Gabriel, but he tried to remain calm. "What happened to Lewis and Jalin?"

Simon didn't want to answer. It was as if the beasts were compelling him from afar to keep quiet. But Gabriel stood there staring and Simon couldn't stand the intense scrutiny any longer. He jumped out of the corner. "I set them up!" he blurted out. "I set them up!"

Gabriel's mouth was agape and he felt sick to his stomach. "You did what?"

"I tricked them," muttered Simon. "After you and the others escaped, I stepped outside the log. The beasts spotted me and blocked my way, then I told them how everyone had escaped and that Lewis and Jalin were still inside. I don't know why I did it, but I did. And I *remember* doing it, even though I can't recall meeting the beasts at night beyond the wall." Simon nervously scratched behind his ears. "Two of the beasts remained and waited on either end of the log while the rest chased after you and the others. I went back inside the log and told Lewis and Jalin that all the beasts had left. They were overjoyed." Simon found it difficult to speak but forced himself to utter each dreadful word. "I exited the log first and told them to follow so we could rejoin the group. They scurried out—but never saw the two beasts attack. Lewis and Jalin didn't have a chance. I ran straight for the wall as fast as I could."

"I remember you sprinting past me like a cold wind," Gabriel said, recalling that awful time.

"So do I," Simon uttered, and then he collapsed and sobbed. "What have I done?"

Gabriel looked on with shame and sympathy. He knew Simon wasn't the friend he had known long ago. Like Livingston, Gabriel realized that the true Simon was gone forever.

"Don't cry, Simon. I—" But Gabriel didn't know what to say. The shock of learning that Simon had betrayed Lewis and Jalin left his senses reeling.

"There's something else, Gabriel." Simon spoke with a raspy voice. "I think I may have met with the beasts once before. Many days ago."

"When?"

"While we were at the frog pond. On the night before our journey to the estate. I had a dream about the beasts then too, or at least I thought it was a dream," Simon said with a heavy sigh. "In the dream I told them every detail about our upcoming journey here. I revealed all the information Greenback and Long Legs had provided us."

"In a *dream*?" Gabriel asked skeptically.

"When I awoke, I was far away from the pond. I was just outside the edge of the woods, so I guess it *couldn't* have been a dream. But I wasn't sure then," Simon said unconvincingly. "Maybe I just tried to make myself believe that I wasn't sure."

"Why didn't you tell us?" Gabriel snapped, trying to control his anger. "We could have changed our plans. *Now* I know how the

123

beasts were able to follow us. They knew where we were headed before we left. You betrayed us all, Simon! Why?"

"I didn't know I was telling them our plans until after it happened, Gabriel. You've got to believe me!"

"Then you should have told me once you realized what you had done."

"How could I? How could I admit doing such a terrible deed to my friends?"

Gabriel shook his head. "Instead you only made the situation worse. Maybe we could have helped if only you trusted us. As you said, we were your friends, Simon. You should have *trusted* us!"

"I know," said Simon, his voice cracking. He turned his back to Gabriel, his shoulders slumped. "Maybe you ought to leave. Please. I don't know what I'll do, but I've got to think. Besides, I'm sure you don't want me around you right now or perhaps ever. No one will once they find out what I've done."

"I can't imagine the others will act kindly when they discover the truth," Gabriel said flatly. "But I won't tell anyone yet. The party is tonight and such horrible news would spoil everybody's good time. They're so looking forward to this night. The truth can wait an extra day."

"Thank you," Simon said as he lay down.

Gabriel watched him silently, unable to absorb all he had just learned. Part of him couldn't believe it—another part of him didn't want to. But Gabriel knew he would have to come to terms with the sad truth sooner than he'd like. He started to exit the hole, his nose inching out into the cool morning air. Sapphire blue skies above cradled wispy strands of clouds and green tree tops. Not fully understanding why he did so, Gabriel stepped back inside and spoke to Simon from the entrance.

"The reason I stopped by was to see if you wanted to go to the party tonight with Violet and me. We thought you could use the company." Simon remained silent. "If you'd still like to go... Well..." Gabriel wished now that he had just left, but tried to make the best of it. "Maybe if you sleep through the day, you'll feel better later. Violet and I will be watching from under the shrubbery closest to the oak tree on the side of the house. You're welcome to meet us there if you'd like."

Simon muttered something, but Gabriel was unsure whether that was an acceptance or just another sigh. He absentmindedly scratched at the ground.

"Tomorrow we'll talk and see if maybe there's a way to, uh—figure out how to help you," Gabriel continued uncomfortably. "But let's try to keep together tonight. Sundown by the shrubbery. Meet us there. Promise?"

"I promise," Simon whispered, his eyes closed. "Maybe things will look different tomorrow."

"Maybe." Gabriel took a last glance at Simon before he headed out of the hole. "I'll see you at sundown then," he added, without looking back.

The guests arrived early in the afternoon, flocking to the estate in droves and dressed in fine summer attire. They mingled outdoors and enjoyed delicious appetizers and refreshing drinks. Laughter and music drifted through the air as the end-of-the-summer party kicked off to a terrific start.

The mice knew they must wait till dusk before indulging in a feast of their own. But that didn't stop them from hiding out in the nearby bushes and tall grass to watch the festivities. Occasionally a guest would accidentally drop a few crumbs of cake or bread, or even a whole cracker, while strolling across the grounds away from the main crowd. A lucky mouse or two could then have a quick snack if nobody was around to notice. But this was a rare treat and several hours still lay between now and their twilight celebration.

"I've never been so restless in my life!" Elmer said while hiding amid a bed of marigolds with several others. "I can smell the food already."

"Patience," Toby advised. "Our time will come soon enough. Maybe you ought to go home and return at dusk if you're that impatient."

"I agree!" another mouse chimed in. "Give up your prime spot so I can have a better look."

"Not a chance," Elmer replied. "I can put up with the delay as well as anybody."

"Do you think there'll be mushrooms again this year?" a mouse whispered from back of the crowd. "I hope so! I could eat mushrooms every day."

"Oh, quiet!" another said. "You're making me *so* hungry. More watching, less talking!"

Similar conversations took place among the mice at various locations on the estate. And though time seemed to drag by at a snail's pace, the sun still cut its daily arc across the sky in due time and finally sank below the purple and red skies along the western horizon.

That's when the strings of lights blazed at their finest. Red, blue, green, yellow and orange bulbs warmly glowed in the summer night in concert with the emerging ice-white stars. Soft jazzy notes from a trumpet and saxophone filled the air, and the voices and laughter of partygoers sounded sharper as the daylight waned.

Beneath the shrubbery near the oak tree on the side of the house, Gabriel waited with Violet by his side. With them were Chester, Florence and several other mice, all anticipating the grand banquet just ahead.

"This is exciting!" Florence said, sniffing the air. "The aromas are so wonderful that I can almost taste the food."

"Save some for us," Gabriel joked, nudging Violet and winking at her.

Violet smiled back. "I'll admit I'm just as delighted as Florence," she said. "We never had such an event in the field. To think what we missed."

"Well, at least *something* good came out of all the trouble those beasts created," Chester added. "If they never bothered us, then we wouldn't be here waiting to enjoy this feast."

"Not funny at all," Florence admonished Chester with a scowl. "Not funny at all. Curses on those beasts!"

"I agree," Gabriel said. "No feast can compensate for all the grief they've caused us." Then he thought about Simon and wondered if he would meet them here as he promised. He took Violet aside. "Maybe I should run back to see if Simon's going to join us."

"Didn't he say he would?" Violet asked.

"He did, but… You know, Simon. He's not thinking properly these days." Gabriel couldn't imagine a way to break the news to the other mice about what Simon had done. Had they known the truth, Simon would be the last mouse they would want foraging next to them at the feast. But that could wait till tomorrow. "I'll check on him fast and be right back, with or without Simon."

"All right, Gabriel," Violet said. "But do hurry. The bell will be rung at any moment."

So Gabriel scurried to Simon's hole beneath the shrubs behind the main house, but was disappointed not to find Simon at home. "He's probably on his way now," Gabriel thought hopefully, though he considered the possibility that Simon might still be upset and had gone off to hide somewhere. Maybe he wouldn't bother to attend the feast at all.

After scouting out the area for a few moments, Gabriel began to worry. The sun had set and a handful of guests had started to file inside. Then the dinner bell clanged seven times, echoing crisply over the grounds. Gabriel decided to return to the others and leave Simon to his own devices. If he really wanted to show up, he knew where to find them.

Gabriel shot across the grass and returned to Violet's side as the last of the dinner guests were walking into the main house. They left behind the dusky grounds littered with food scraps under the warm and colorful lights. The mice's feast was about to begin. Gabriel couldn't wait to dive in, though one question still plagued him. Where was Simon?

Shortly before sunset, Simon had awakened in his hole. He felt refreshed and less agitated after having slept the entire day away. Then he remembered he had promised to meet Gabriel by the side shrubbery in time for the feast. Simon rushed out of his hole and went on his way, cradled in the cool air of approaching twilight. A tangle of dying sun rays lay twisted upon the grass.

The string lights glowed warmly near the main house. Simon spotted them at once, eager to bathe in their comforting illumination. He was especially fascinated with the green bulbs and paused now and then, staring at them dreamily. As he passed the oak tree on his way to the side shrubbery, the clang of the dinner bell rent the still evening air. Simon watched as the guests drifted inside. He was right on time.

The shrubbery grew several yards away, so Simon hurried to join Gabriel and Violet. But as he swished through the cool grass, he thought he heard a gentle voice call to him. Simon stopped, stood on his hind legs, and listened. Thin voices drifted through the dusky air and found him.

"*Remember, Simon,*" they eerily whispered. "*Remember the plan.*"

"Who's that?" Simon demanded. But he heard no reply so continued on.

Yet the voices persisted, growing louder and closer. Were they real or only in his mind? Simon stopped again and listened, scanning the area, hoping to determine from which direction they originated.

"Who's there? Who's calling me?" snapped Simon.

Then the tone of the voices grew more demanding and strident. *Remember the plan!* Simon felt dizzy and began to feel wobbly in the legs. The lights in the distance seemed to dance in the air then slowly fade—except for the green lights. As Simon watched, they grew brighter and brighter in his eyes and seemed as big as limes. *Remember the plan!* He still heard the voices like a crash of angry waves against a rocky seashore. His mind was a jumble of sound and images, none of which made any sense. All thoughts of joining Gabriel and Violet beneath the shrubbery had vanished in the confusion.

"I'm here," Simon whispered flatly, looking in the direction of the main gate. The voices commanded him to approach. Simon tore off towards the gate like a lightning flash, eager to be on the other side. His friends and the feast were a distant memory.

Simon stood at the base of the metal gate as the last of the dinner guests disappeared inside the house. He watched as the side door closed and the lawns were left deserted. Simon suddenly felt alert and full of energy as he slipped underneath the gate and dashed towards Major Grump's chicken wire pen. The Major, having consumed a large meal of his own, slept soundly within his dog house beneath the sprawling oak. Simon had no fear of the dog now.

He surveyed the pen, scurrying back and forth along the base. Then Simon stopped in front of the gate and climbed up the chicken wire till he reached the wooden latch on the pen door. He grasped the latch with both front claws, trying to turn it to open the gate. The shadows of twilight deepened and several black forms gathered below, churning and twirling in a controlled frenzy. Simon looked down and saw six pairs of glowing green eyes moving erratically back and forth like slithering snakes. He heard whispers and hisses and snarls reverberate in his head. The beasts had arrived. The moment was at hand.

"Hurry, Simon!" the leader commanded, his eyes burning like fire. "Open the gate. Open it at once!"

"I'm trying!" Simon said, struggling with the latch. He grasped onto the chicken wire to keep from falling.

The restless beasts below cursed at the delay as they swirled in the darkness. Some grew angry and began to jump against the pen, fruitlessly trying to break through. But just before their wrath exploded, Simon released the latching mechanism and the gate swung open.

The beasts rushed into the pen like charging horses, knocking the fence post so violently that Simon was thrown off and tumbled through the air. He landed squarely on top of the leader of the beasts and clutched onto its mangy fur for dear life as it sped through the night.

The six beasts slipped past Major Grump who remained in a deep sleep. Then, one by one, they climbed the oak tree till they reached a large branch extending over the estate wall. Like a swift but invisible breeze, the six darted across the branch in single file, blending in with the deadly darkness, save for their wickedly glowing eyes. Simon held his breath and closed his eyes as he was not used to such heights.

The oak branch extended over a lower roof of the main house and the beasts jumped onto it without a sound. Quickly they gathered at the edge of the roof, surveyed the area below, and then followed their leader in a short jump onto the slanted roof below. They clambered down this section till they reached the roof of a small stone porch on the far side of the house.

The distance to the ground was now only eight feet. Each of the beasts leaped off the porch roof and landed on the grass unharmed. Simon closed his eyes even tighter when the leader jumped and for a moment felt he was flying like a bird. He enjoyed the sensation and a part of him felt glad to be among the beasts instead of with the mice. But Simon had no more time to think, for in the next instant the leader sputtered a hideous command to the others and tore off into the shadows. The beasts followed close behind, with eyes blazing and teeth bared, prepared to hunt down the mice.

The moment finally arrived. As if a single thought had instructed them, the mice converged onto the lawn from their hiding places under the shrubbery, behind the rocks and among the tall grass and flowers. They scattered under the tables and chairs and along the patio, searching out every cracker crumb and cheese cube, each pretzel stick or scrap of meat. Every item of food was greedily devoured. Even a few paper cups of sweet tasting drinks lay about, and the mice lapped up the contents in delight. Several birds and a few squirrels joined in the outdoor feast. There was plenty for everyone.

"Didn't I tell you this would be the most wonderful evening of the year?" Toby commented to Gabriel as he gnawed at an unopened peanut shell. "We'll have hours to feast at our leisure before anybody returns!"

Gabriel replied with a contented squeak as he and Violet nibbled away at a buttered roll that had fallen beneath one of the tables. Each grinned at the other as they enjoyed their banquet under the stars.

"I'm ready for seconds!" Chester said after gulping down half a rolled up piece of Swiss cheese and a wheat cracker.

"I'm already on *thirds*!" Elmer replied.

"Pace yourself," Edmund cautioned them. "Remember to save some food for leaner times. Cold weather is not far off, and winter's fury will close in on us shortly after."

"Well it's still summer where I'm standing," Florence said. "And I plan to enjoy every morsel of this meal even if I burst! Now less talking and more eating, please."

Dozens of mice scoured the lawn diligently, not letting even the tiniest crumb escape their notice. They planned to dine for an hour or so, and then would begin to take some of the scraps back to their homes and hoard them for the breezy and crimson days of autumn. Nobody had a care this evening. All wished the warm and wonderful night would never end.

Then they heard it—terrible growls and sinister hisses near the azalea bush around the corner of the house. Everyone looked up, frozen in terror. Suddenly the beasts attacked, riding in like black thunder clouds, charging at the mice, leaping over chairs and tables, and ripping down the strings of colorful lights. Saliva dripped from the sharp points of their teeth. The mice squealed and shot in every direction seeking cover. Their tiny hearts pounded and their minds swam in confusion. This couldn't be happening! Of all nights, not on *this* night! But the beasts were indeed within the grounds of the estate, tracking the mice in relentless pursuit.

"Run for your lives!" Edmund warned, the first mouse to snap to his senses. "The beasts are attacking! The beasts are attacking!"

"We're doomed!" Toby cried. "Doomed!"

"Save us!" another voice wailed before suddenly going silent under an approaching shadow.

At first sight of the beasts, Gabriel raced to Violet and led her back to the side shrubbery as fast as his legs could go. "Stay close to me, Violet! Don't leave my side."

"This is horrible, Gabriel! What'll we do?" she said, her limbs shaking.

When the pair found safety under the shrubs, they watched in helpless dread as the beasts chased several of their companions across the lawn, mercilessly tearing up the grass and flowers. Within the first few moments of the attack, four mice lay dead near one of the canopies, and the sparrow Gabriel had met the other day was killed by one of the beasts before it could fly over the stone wall.

Florence would have been a victim herself were it not for the bravery of Chester and Elmer. At the first sign of trouble, Florence ran towards her home, but one of the beasts spotted her and gave chase. She gritted her teeth and scurried through the grass, the world a blur. Just as the beast's powerful paw was about to strike her down, Chester and Elmer leaped out from a nearby bush and lunged at the beast's right hind leg as it passed by. The two brothers dug their sharp claws and teeth into the creature till it screamed. It stopped instantly and spun around, writhing in pain. Chester and Elmer were flung through the air into a clump of marigolds and barely escaped with their lives. Florence, in the meantime, rushed back to the security inside her hole.

Gabriel and Violet, meanwhile, scanned the area to see if the way was safe for them to flee back home. They breathed heavily in the cool night air, burning with fear and uncertainty.

"I think it's safe to go," Gabriel whispered. "I don't hear any noise nearby."

"Maybe we should stay here?" Violet suggested, clutching onto Gabriel. "I'm so scared."

"Me too," Gabriel admitted. "But I don't think we should remain much longer. I don't feel safe. Now that the beasts are inside the estate grounds, they'll search under every shrub and among all the flower beds. It's only a matter of time till they find us."

"All right, Gabriel. I trust you to do the right thing. You'll get us out of this mess if anyone can," Violet whispered in his ear. "I *know* you will."

Uplifted by Violet's confidence in him, Gabriel poked his nose out of the shrubbery and sensed all was safe for the moment. Noises from the attack were still audible in the distance. Gabriel signaled for Violet to follow, and then the two tore off towards his hole. They were almost there, speeding around the back corner of the house, nearly home free, when a large black figure jumped out from behind a tree. The beast emitted a deadly hiss as it swung one of its razor-sharp claws, just grazing Gabriel's back. Gabriel screamed in pain and nearly fainted, but forced himself to keep up with Violet as she took refuge behind the base of a stone birdbath just ahead. Gabriel joined her and both watched helplessly as the beast stopped running and slowly approached. A pair of fiery green eyes floated in the darkness.

The beast breathed down, its breath hot and stale. Gabriel inched around the base of the birdbath, keeping Violet behind him all the while. His back burned with pain where he had been scratched. Trickles of warm blood dotted his chestnut-brown fur. Though tired and frightened, and nearly mesmerized when looking at the beast, Gabriel snapped out of his stupor in shock at what he saw next. High atop the beast in the thickening shadows, clutching its fur and baring his teeth, sat his old friend Simon. Gabriel wanted to doubt his eyes but couldn't. Simon, however, didn't seem to recognize Gabriel, and merely looked past him as if he were invisible. Gabriel knew in his heart that Simon was truly dead.

"I can't believe…" was all Gabriel managed to utter.

"I can't either," Violet softly said, feeling their end was near.

As they circled around the birdbath, Gabriel knew that the beast was toying with them, making them sweat out their last moments before it attacked. He and Violet were too weak to run much farther and had little chance to outrun the beast again even if they tried. Their nearest refuge was in a thicket of rose bushes, but that was *behind* the beast and there was no way to reach it from this spot without going around the creature.

"I'm scared, Gabriel! I don't know what to do!"

"Stay close to me, Violet. Just promise me that."

In the next instant, Gabriel saw the beast slightly bend its hind legs and knew it was about to pounce. Their time was up. If only he had taken a different path, Gabriel thought as the beast raised its thin body. If only Violet could at least live, he hoped as the beast was framed against the silhouette of the rose bushes. If only…

Then it struck Gabriel in the split second before the beast made its deadly leap. There *was* a way.

"Do exactly what I do!" Gabriel whispered to Violet as the beast seemed to grow like a rising tidal wave.

Then it jumped through the air towards the base of the birdbath, directly at Gabriel and Violet. But instead of running away to one side or the other, Gabriel gathered his last remnants of courage and ran straight at the beast, bolting directly underneath him with Violet right behind. The two slipped safely inside the rose bushes just as the beast landed near the birdbath, tearing at the grass in a fit of heated rage.

The creature spun around and screeched. It craned its scrawny neck in every conceivable angle, sniffing the air as its green eyes darted in search of its prey. The chase wasn't over yet—not by a long shot. With its back arched and its fur standing on end, the beast raced through the grass, determined to find the two mice who had tricked him and hunt them down with a vengeance.

Major Grump, in the meantime, had been roused from his sleep and sniffed at the cool night air, sensing trouble. His ears pricked up when he heard the turmoil on the other side of the stone wall. When the Major's weary eyes caught sight of the pen gate wide open, his heart beat wildly and he scrambled out of his quarters with all the grace of a charging elephant. His sharp barks pierced the night as he jumped against the front iron gate, desperately trying to get inside. The screams of the beasts and the squeaks of the frightened mice drove him into a frenzy. Soon the dinner guests were aware of the distraction and hurried outdoors. Several gasped at the sight of the tumbled chairs and ripped strings of lights hanging like dying vines. The beasts, however, ignored the spectators and continued their vicious assault.

Moments later, amid the caterwauls and confusion, several shotgun blasts echoed across the countryside. The dinner guests hushed. Major Grump ceased his barking and was led back to the chicken wire pen. The mice were nowhere in sight, having swiftly taken shelter in the nearby shrubbery and tall grass. Crickets chirped madly on the other side of the wall as the first quarter moon drifted across the sky, casting icy shadows. Sprawled out among the cool grass on the side of the main house, five of the six beasts lay dead.

CHAPTER NINETEEN

Hide and Seek

Gabriel and Violet sprinted through the grass under a moonlit sky. Their hearts pounded like drums and their lungs burned with each breath. Every limb and muscle cried out for rest, but the two dared not stop even for an instant while in the open. They fled the safety the rose bushes had provided moments after taking refuge there, fearing to stay so close to the beast. Gabriel and Violet could still hear the creature in its dogged pursuit, with Simon clinging to the scruff of its neck. Gabriel wondered what twisted thoughts occupied his former friend's mind at this horrid moment.

A circle of slender birch trees offered Gabriel and Violet a brief rest. They disappeared inside a bed of ivy blanketing the ground at the base of the trees and collapsed. Moonlight illuminated the white paper-like bark peeling off the tree trunks. They were safe for a moment.

"If only we were back home in the field," Violet whispered to Gabriel, snuggled up to his side. "With Simon and Livingston both as alive and carefree as they used to be." Her voice quavered in fear. "If only those creatures were simply part of a bad dream."

135

"Those are a lot of *if onlys* to consider," Gabriel said, trying to comfort her. "And I don't think there's much I can do to make them come true." He gazed into her clover-green eyes sparkling with a ray of moonlight slipping inside the ivy patch. "However, if only we survive this horrible night, then I promise to stay with you always and love you, and never let anything ever harm you." Gabriel gulped, feeling as tall as a squirrel yet uncertain as a leaf fluttering in the wind. "That is, if it's okay with *you*, Violet. I mean, if you want me hanging around—"

"It is! And I *do*, Gabriel!" Violet nuzzled her nose to his and squeaked. "Stay with me always, Gabriel, from this day to the end. I couldn't imagine a better way to spend my life."

"Neither can I," he said flashing a broad far-away smile, as if swimming blithely in a pleasant daydream he wanted never to end.

Then both mice dropped like rocks back into reality. A nearby noise. A low growl. A swishing of grass. The creature prowled just outside the circle of ivy.

"It's back!" Violet whispered, clutching Gabriel. He nodded and indicated for her not to make a sound.

The beast slowly circled the birch trees, sniffing at the edges of the ivy that gently flowed out from the base of the tree trunks, pawing among its outer leafy tendrils. The creature hissed through sharp teeth while slinking round and round the trees, certain that Gabriel and Violet were tucked inside the undergrowth. Simon, still in a daze, remained silent atop the creature, clutching on for dear life.

Gabriel and Violet, hidden in the center of the ivy, could see through the web of leaves exactly where the creature stood. The two mice turned in a slow circle as they followed the progress of the creature in its taunting performance. Slowly, step by careful step, the beast walked lazy rings around the arrangement of trees as it analyzed its next move. Thinking, debating, deciding...

The beast stopped. It had determined where it would leap into the ivy to catch its prey and put an end to this endless chase.

And Gabriel knew it. As soon as the creature stopped moving, he felt a sickening chill clutch his body and knew he and Violet would have to run again. He looked at her for the briefest moment and knew that she understood the situation too. It was time to leave. Now.

The creature, poised on the west side of the circle, meticulously sniffed the air above the top of the ivy leaves as it slowly leaned back on its hind legs. Gabriel, anticipating this exact moment, fled with Violet out of the east side of the tree ring and raced for home just as the beast sprang into the air.

It landed with a thump right in the middle of the circle of birch trees, ripping away at the ivy in search of a prey that was no longer there. The beast screeched and hissed with bitter disappointment as it flailed about, nearly knocking Simon off its back. But in a flash it was again in pursuit, not easily defeated and still relishing a spirited chase.

"I can't take—much more—of this," Violet said between gasps for breath.

"No choice!" Gabriel insisted. "We're nearly home."

But he found no joy in those words because he could hear the creature closing in on them again. As he and Violet tore through the grass, he knew they'd never reach home safely if they tried to make a straight line for it. His hole under the back shrubbery was too far away to reach with a beast gaining fast. He needed a new strategy immediately. Then like magic, riding on a cool breeze, Gabriel heard it. The steady and unconcerned croaking of frogs filled the air as thick as fireflies in July. The garden pond! He and Violet could take refuge there just as he and Simon had done in the field so many weeks ago. The pond was much closer than his home, so Gabriel made a great arc across the lawn and headed for the water, filling in Violet on his plan as they raced for their lives.

Though the garden pond sported a few patches of cattails and sprouted a generous amount of tall grass along its edge, it couldn't boast of the seemingly limitless plant life that blossomed around the pond back in the field. So Gabriel knew that he and Violet would be safe here only for a short while before the creature would nose them out. Still, they'd have enough time to catch their breath, drink some water and plan the next stage of an escape.

They hid in a clump of cattails on the water's edge and gulped greedily from the pond. The first quarter moon pasted its silver reflection on the smooth surface. Neither mouse said a word till they had drunk their fill, yet both wondered how the other mice were faring back near the party area.

Violet looked up a few moments later, about to speak, when they heard another noise far away. Major Grump barked up a storm near the front of the estate. The beasts, undoubtedly, had awakened the dog, and the Major definitely did not enjoy interruptions to his sleep.

Suddenly several loud booms split the still night of the countryside like fiery cracks of lightning. Gabriel and Violet stood on their hind legs, ears pricked, sniffing the air. Neither could imagine what had just happened, but everything sounded uncomfortably quiet moments afterward.

"What was *that*?" Violet asked, hoping Gabriel could offer even the tiniest bit of an explanation.

But he merely scratched behind his ear, his eyes filled with bewilderment. "I couldn't begin to tell you, Violet. But something *has* happened. Something *big*. Whether we're safer here or there, though, remains to be seen."

"I'll only feel safe when the sun rises high in tomorrow's sky, Gabriel. This is the worst night of my life," Violet said, trying not to cry. "Our lives here weren't supposed to be like this."

Gabriel gently rubbed the back of his claw along the side of her face, offering a hint of an awkward smile to cheer her. "I don't know how our life is supposed to be, Violet, but I'm eager to find out once this business is over. We'll get through this ordeal," he uttered with confidence. "We will! Trust me."

"I do trust you," she replied, expelling a deep breath. "Just tell me what we should do next. I'll try anything to get out of this mess."

"That's the spirit!" Gabriel winked at Violet and snapped his tail. "We'll leave here as soon as we can. But first I need to check our bearings and see if our *friend* is anywhere in sight."

"Where are you going?" Violet asked in alarm.

"Just taking a peek through the cattails. Don't be frightened."

"Be careful, Gabriel."

"I will. Maybe we gave that beast the slip this time," he said with hope.

Gabriel smiled at Violet then merged into the cattails and crawled towards the edge. He poked his nose outside, but all that greeted his eyes was the black of night. Dense as coal dust. Inky as the inside of the deepest cave. The night had grown deadly dark. Gabriel looked up to catch a glimpse of the moon and stars and was happy to see them still shining far above. Then two other stars appeared closer to the horizon, suddenly springing to life, colorful, shiny and green.

Gabriel nearly collapsed in a cold and clammy pile. The two stars were not stars at all, but a pair of glowing green eyes. And they were not far off on the horizon but directly in front of him, set in the mountain of blackness squatting on the ground straight ahead. The beast had discovered their hiding spot!

Gabriel squealed and fell backwards as the beast leaped at him. He managed to scramble back down to the edge of the water where Violet waited, just ahead of the line of cattails that snapped and cracked apart as the beast methodically ripped through their woody stems. Inch by inch it moved closer to the mice.

Violet knew what had happened as soon as Gabriel returned to her side all out of breath. "This is really it!" she said, resigned to the awful fate awaiting them.

They stared at one another, knowing what a fix they were in. Trapped at the water's edge as the beast, only a few steps away, continued to lay down a path of destruction. But Gabriel knew he couldn't simply stand there with Violet at his side and await death. He couldn't have it end this way. There was only one thing to do.

"He doesn't have us yet!" Gabriel sputtered with mounting indignation. "If that beast wants us, he'll have to work for it! Into the water!"

"What? We can't swim, Gabriel!"

"We won't have to. Follow my lead."

Without a second thought, Gabriel led Violet into the cold pond water till it was nearly up to their heads. Then they grabbed onto the edge of an enormous lily pad, clambering up its slippery side with each dig of their claws into the fleshy plant. After a tiring struggle, both finally plopped on top of the wavy pad, wet, tired and chilled to the bone. The lily pad slowly drifted away from shore towards the center of the pond.

When the beast finally poked its head through the cattails, with eyes blazing and fangs bared, it pounded its paws upon the shore and into the water's edge, searching for the mice, not realizing that Gabriel and Violet had drifted away. The waves it created sent the two mice farther and faster across the water. When the beast eventually saw the pair floating off in the moonlight, it cried shrilly and smashed at the water harder, sending even more waves that pushed the mice well beyond its reach. Gabriel and Violet sailed safely across the starlit pond.

"I think we're safe," Gabriel said, dripping wet. Though he could still detect the blackened shape of the beast at the edge of the pond, he and Violet were well out of danger. "That good-for-nothing scoundrel doesn't know who he's dealing with!" Gabriel spouted with bravado, feeling like he could outwit every beast in the countryside.

"I'll never doubt your word, Gabriel. Never." Violet broke into a wide grin as she glanced at the moon. "I only hope the others are faring as well as we are."

"I hope so too. Say, look!" Gabriel said excitedly, carefully standing on his feet and gazing at the edge of the pond. "The beast is giving up. See? It's moving back through the cattails. Looks like we'll be okay after all."

Like a passing storm cloud, the shadowy outline of the creature swiftly departed, disappearing into the cattails from the direction in which it attacked. Gabriel turned to Violet and grinned with satisfaction. He couldn't possibly feel any better than at this moment.

Nor any worse than in the next.

The clumps of grass and cattails scattered around the pond swished and wavered in the moonlight as something ran furiously through them. A throaty croaking of frogs punctuated the unsettling sounds. Gabriel and Violet spun around and eyed the other end of the pond that grew nearer as the lily pad floated towards it. Except for a bloom of cattails, the area at that end lay deserted. Then all went silent. The movement in the plants had ceased. Even the frogs seemed to have quieted. Suddenly the beast reappeared, crawling out of the cattails and standing on the opposite edge of the pond as still as stone, waiting silently while Gabriel and Violet drifted helplessly towards it.

Violet gasped and clutched onto Gabriel, her body shaking. The advantage of their clever, last-minute escape had now turned into their doom. The mice were sailing straight into the enemy's grasp and there was nothing they could do to stop it.

"Gabriel..." Violet whispered his name, her strength and spirit draining from her.

"I see it," Gabriel said, his chest tightening and his mind in a jumble. All he could think about was saving Violet when they reached the end of the pond. *His* safety didn't matter. Perhaps if he immediately charged at the beast, then Violet would have a few moments to run and hide and return home when she found a chance. It seemed the only option, and the only honorable thing to do.

As they drifted closer and closer to the beast, Violet clung tightly to Gabriel and closed her eyes, but Gabriel faced the menace with a mix of horror and wonder. He studied the creature's haggard face and fiery green eyes as it stood motionless and silent, like a volcano waiting to erupt. Slowly, Gabriel's dread was replaced by an eager curiosity. He stared fixedly at his adversary and began to think that the creature had a peculiar yet pleasant appeal about it after all.

"There's nothing to fear," it whispered over the water. A pair of glowing eyes served as a beacon in the night. "Come join us. We'll lead you far from this place to a much better home."

Gabriel found the words alluring and found no argument to counter them. Maybe he had misjudged the beasts. Maybe they were nothing like the loathsome wretches he had always imagined. What new worlds could he conquer standing at their side?

"Don't listen to him!" Violet said, seeing the dazed look in Gabriel's eyes. She grabbed the fur behind his neck and shook him. "The beast is only trying to deceive you by putting you under its spell."

The beast softly laughed. "Join us. Both of you! There is nothing to fear and so much to gain." It tilted its head slightly and looked behind his shoulder. "Your friend up here has already learned the truth, and welcomes the triumphs that await. Join us!"

Gabriel noticed the small dark lump on top of the beast. He strained his eyes to get a better look and smiled when seeing his dear old friend.

"Simon! So you're still with us!" he cried joyfully. "I'm glad to see you're all right. I'll join you as soon as I reach shore."

Simon said nothing, however, wearing the same glazed, far-away expression that was slowly consuming Gabriel.

"A wise mouse," the beast said. "Indeed, Simon and I know what's best for you."

As they floated closer to shore, Gabriel never took his eyes off the creature, though Violet tried to shake him out of his hypnotic trance. Feelings of unknown happiness welled up inside Gabriel, and he wondered why he had ever hated the beasts. He couldn't wait to meet one.

"Listen to me, Gabriel!" Violet shouted in his ear. "Pay attention, you waterlogged fool!"

"We'll both be fine, Violet. Trust me," Gabriel lazily replied.

"No we won't," she said. "We need help!"

But it was too late. The lily pad floated to the edge of the shore and stopped. Gabriel crawled off the fleshy pad though Violet tried pulling him back. The beast stood less than three feet away—a mountain of trouble under the starry sky. Gabriel ambled slowly towards the creature who waited patiently for him to approach. It wanted Gabriel to willingly walk the short distance to his doom.

"Don't leave without me," Gabriel whispered, his eyes fixed on the beast. "Please don't leave!"

"Don't intend to," it uttered with a false sweetness that sickened Violet.

And though she tugged and tugged at Gabriel and demanded that he snap out of it, Violet only slowed his progress. At any moment they would be in striking range of the creature should it wish to take a deadly swipe at them, though right now it merely wanted to torment the mice.

The beast's bony and haggard face grew grimmer in the shadows. Gabriel's legs felt heavier and heavier, and each footstep seemed more difficult than the last. He thought he heard Violet's voice urgently trying to tell him something. And though he couldn't take his eyes off the creature, its soothing whispers now sounded abrasive and chilling. Gabriel wondered why Simon sat on top of the beast when he should be home with the others.

"Hurry!" the beast demanded, noticing that Gabriel and Violet were resisting. "Come to me at once!"

It could easily strike both of them down in an instant, but the creature wanted the mice to voluntarily walk those final steps before it dealt out their fate. The beast desired to possess Gabriel and Violet's total trust and devotion for one instant—*then* kill them.

Gabriel slowly realized this as the pleasant sounds from the creature turned grating and hollow. He heard Violet's voice now, clearer and stronger, as he tried to shake off the beast's spell still tugging at his mind and heart. But as much as he wanted to break away, Gabriel couldn't prevent himself from moving forward into the jaws of despair and death. He couldn't save himself. He couldn't save Violet. And Simon was already beyond saving. Gabriel sadly realized that this was truly the end.

"Now you will find out how powerful I really am!" the beast snarled as it rose to its fullest height. "Now you good-for-nothing mice will learn what happens when you attempt to defy forces you cannot defeat!"

The creature's green eyes glowed like a sickly fire as it raised its foreleg. With sharp claws extended like knives, it prepared to deliver a lethal swipe to Gabriel. Violet refused to leave his side and resigned herself to share his bitter fate. But as the beast set to strike, a dark shape bounded out of the cattails and sailed high overhead, boxing the creature in one ear with a wet foot before landing with a splash in the water.

"Long live the storyteller!" shouted Widefoot, as the huge slimy frog sent a splash of water into the eyes of the beast.

"Save our furry friends!" cried Leaper, who closely followed Widefoot, directing a second slap of water right at the beast.

Gabriel and Violet, also soaked from the frogs' surprise landing, stumbled backwards as the beast screeched in anger, its deadly swipe missing its mark.

Suddenly more dark shapes soared through the air from out of the cattails, and still more and more—all landing with terrific splashes into the pond and sending explosions of water in the direction of the beast. The creature quickly retreated in a blind fury, sputtering and hissing, wiping the pond water out of its stinging eyes.

Gabriel, after receiving another spray of water in his face, snapped back to reality. His mind cleared and his limbs felt on fire. The strange voices had left his head. He quickly grabbed hold of Violet before she could say a word and led her through the tall grass in the direction away from the beast. The paratrooping frogs continued to dive-bomb the pond, bombarding the shoreline with raisin-size drops of water amid their shouts of defiance against the beast.

Then, just as quickly as the frogs had emerged from their hiding places in the cattails and jumped into the pond, they were gone. In unison, they dived underwater and left the pond still and silent, with the quarter moon again reflecting coolly on its mirrored surface. But their job was successfully completed, giving Gabriel and Violet time to escape. The beast, however, only temporarily disoriented, howled in rage as it tore through the cattails and resumed its chase.

Gabriel and Violet simply ran, not caring which direction they headed. As they neared the back stone wall, the alarming noise of swishing grass caught their ears again. They knew without a doubt that the beast was still in pursuit.

"I can't run anymore, Gabriel! My legs are dead tired," Violet said, feeling as if she were stuck in the haunting blackness of a horrible dream.

"We may not have to run anymore, Violet. I think we're approaching the back wall," Gabriel said. "I have an idea."

"Anything! As long as we can stop!"

"Hurry and follow me. This might work!"

Gabriel led Violet past the rotting wooden well cover lying nearby, slowly being consumed by tall grass and time. Then he paused at the base of the stone well, breathing heavily. Violet looked up in disbelief.

"You expect us to scale this mountain, I suppose?"

"Sure. I've already climbed up there twice," Gabriel said matter-of-factly. "I'm hoping the beast won't know we're on top, and it'll give us a terrific vantage point to see everything below. We'll know the instant it gives up the chase and slinks away."

"*If* it gives up," Violet added skeptically. "I don't ever think we'll be safe here again."

"Well no time to debate that point," Gabriel said. "Up we go. We have no choice, Violet."

She reluctantly agreed and cautiously clambered up the side of the well next to Gabriel, step by weary step, feeling for a foothold in the stones, daring not to look down for fear of getting dizzy and losing her balance. Once or twice she nearly lost her grip, but Violet managed to hold on through sheer determination and a few encouraging words from Gabriel.

At last they scrambled up and over the last stone and dropped in exhaustion on the slate rim of the well. For a few moments Gabriel didn't even think about the prowling beast below because he was so tired. All he wanted to do was close his eyes and sleep. Violet expressed a similar desire, but after a little recovery time, both mice struggled to their feet.

"Wait here," Gabriel said, before scurrying around the well to survey the area. He saw no sign of the creature which cheered him only slightly. Maybe they *had* fooled the beast this time.

He returned to Violet and stood close to her, their hearts beating wildly. From a distance they appeared as two small black specks atop a towering fortress, the moonlight shimmering upon their large questioning eyes.

"I think we'll be okay," Gabriel whispered at last, trying to sound upbeat.

"I hope you're right, Gabriel. I really *want* you to be right," Violet replied, still observing the landscape below. Their voices sounded thin and lonely in the cool night air.

Gabriel nuzzled up to Violet, hoping to calm her, then his back suddenly arched and a deadly chill seized him. He scrutinized the ground and thought he saw something move behind the broken well cover. Violet silently indicated that she noticed it too. They watched closely, but nothing stirred. Maybe it was their imagination, but just in case, and without speaking a word, Gabriel signaled that they should tiptoe around to the far side of the well rim as a precaution.

The minutes passed by slowly. Crickets chirped monotonously in the grass as a breeze sailed by carrying a hint of autumn. The stars and quarter moon rambled on along their westward path. All else remained eerily still.

Without warning, an immense shadow blotted out a huge swath of the landscape directly in front of their eyes. Gabriel thought he had lost his sight for an instant, but quickly learned otherwise. He and Violet had moved to the far end of the well just in time. For now on the opposite side, perched on its bony hind legs, sat the snarling beast, with Simon still clutching its fur. It had spotted the two mice from below when near the well cover and leaped up upon the rim. Its green eyes glowed wickedly. Its breath flowed stale and hot across the gaping hole. Slowly, tauntingly, the beast circled.

"Now it's time to join me or die," it hissed. "No more running. No more hiding. You've resisted too long." The creature's eyes didn't blink once, but only stared at Gabriel and Violet like a dim pair of suns through a smog-filled sky. "Come to me as Simon did. Join us and live with the night."

"Never!" Gabriel cried as he inched away from the beast with Violet close to him. He tried with difficulty to keep the creature always on the opposite end of the well. "Go away! Return to the other side of the wall and leave us. We don't want you here." He called to Simon, not knowing if he could hear him speak. "Climb down off of that miserable creature, Simon, and save yourself! Don't be part of its deceit and destruction."

The beast scowled. "Too late! Your *former* friend has wisely chosen sides. He has more sense than both of you. And whether you want it or not, I *am* here, and there's nothing you can do about it, mouse!" The creature sneered at Gabriel's defiance. "Now do as I say! There's no escape this time. Your last chance is *now*!"

"We'd rather die than follow you!" Violet sputtered.

"That can be easily arranged, my dear," uttered the beast, moving faster and faster around the well rim.

Gabriel and Violet scurried as quickly as they could to keep their adversary always opposite them, but the task proved wearisome for the tired mice. The dark surroundings grew dizzying as their pace picked up, and once or twice the beast shifted direction without warning and pursued the pair going the other way. Gabriel knew it was only a matter of time before the beast finally caught them.

He realized that he might never see another sunrise again and recalled the wonderful carefree life in the field with Simon and Livingston. Warm sunny days and food aplenty. Tramping through the grass and along the stream. Seeking out a fresh crop of toad stools and wild raspberries after a warm rain. How good life had been only a short while ago, and Gabriel wished he had it all back. But here on the rim of the well this frightful night, everything teetered on the brink between life and death.

Gabriel glanced up at Simon and felt sorry for his friend, not quite sure where his mind was at the moment. It was probably too late for Simon, he thought, but when he looked at Violet next to him and saw the devotion in her eyes, Gabriel knew he still had much to live for and could not give up. A warm and invigorating wave rushed through him, offering Gabriel one more burst of energy to continue in their race around the well as he again led them safely opposite the beast.

"We won't go with you!" Gabriel shouted amid gasps for breath. "Not ever! Do you hear me? Not ever!"

Instantly the beast stopped, its back arched and its slavering tongue licking the deadly points of its fangs. "I've grown tired of this game and your endless prattle! The chase is over and your time is up. I'll take you both. *Now!*"

The beast lunged across the gaping hole of the well, its claws extended to strike down the mice. Gabriel, grabbing Violet to protect her, reeled back in horror as the black shadow flew at them. The pair wavered on the rim of the well for an instant before losing their balance, and then tumbled off the edge into the grass. The beast screamed at the same instant for Simon had dug his sharp claws into the creature's neck, drawing a trickle of blood.

The beast clumsily landed on the opposite side of the well as it tried to shake Simon off its neck, managing only to grab hold of the outer rim of slate with its two front paws. Its hind legs slipped into the well and the beast tried desperately to climb back onto the rim. The creature clutched onto the slate with its forelegs, its sliding claws fruitlessly trying to dig into the stone. At the same time the beast vainly attempted to get a foothold on the smooth wall of inner rocks with its hind legs.

Simon had nearly fallen off the creature during the leap and was now half awake. His front claws were warm with the blood of the beast, and he tried to remember why he had dug them into the creature's neck. He could vaguely hear the voice of Gabriel echoing in his head and wondered where his friend of old was at the moment. Simon wondered why *he* was slipping inside a well and nearly panicked when he looked down into its black and watery depths. The frightened mouse whimpered and attempted to climb over the head of the beast as it struggled to hoist itself out of the well.

With a sudden burst of strength, Simon scurried between the creature's ears and over its nose and dropped onto the rim of the well. He gazed directly into the beast's blazing eyes as it battled to save itself, and then took a step back. The once powerful and imposing beast looked pathetic and desperate at the moment, and Simon began to question why he had ever sided with it.

"So you're—preparing to—abandon me now, Simon?" the beast grunted, unable to get a foothold and slowly losing its grip. "Save me—as I once saved you!"

Simon shuddered and backed away even farther, having no desire to be with the beast now. Then he heard someone call out his name.

"Jump, Simon!" Gabriel shouted from below. He and Violet looked up at the drama from a tangle of grass. "Jump and save yourself!"

"Hurry!" Violet urged him on. "Please hurry!"

Simon looked upon his old friends and the tiniest bit of hope warmed his icy soul. He couldn't explain what had happened or why he was here, then waves of sorrow suddenly overwhelmed him, and the true horror of what he had done over the past weeks shook his body to the core. He shot a disdainful glance at the beast, no longer mesmerized by its glowing green eyes nor enticed by its empty words. He knew he must get away at once.

The beast knew it too. He hissed at the mouse as it frantically grasped at the well rim, its hind feet scratching against the inner stones as if they were ice.

"You'll never be free of me!" it bellowed out in a last desperate breath. "Do you hear me, traitor? Never!"

Then with a single swipe of its claw, the creature lashed out at Simon before finally losing its grip. Simon squeaked when he saw the beast make a last grab for him and turned to run. He cried out in pain an instant later when he felt the creature's sharp nails dig into the side of his hind leg. Simon was pulled backwards by the beast and the two toppled into the well. Screams of terror filled the night but were instantly cut short, swallowed up in a pool of icy water and razor-sharp rocks.

Gabriel and Violet heard the commotion from the ground and witnessed the dark shapes struggle and drop out of sight. Though still a bit disoriented from their own fall into the grass, the two mice started to climb back up the side of the well to learn the fate of Simon and the beast. Gabriel thought he already knew. The night was as still as an empty house when they reached the top.

"Catch your breath first, Violet," Gabriel whispered when they plopped down on the well rim. He was reluctant to look inside just yet, wanting to prolong the awful truth he knew awaited them. He glanced at the stars for reassurance, then looked at Violet with downcast eyes and nodded slightly. It was time.

Without a word between them, Gabriel and Violet slowly crawled to the inner edge of the well and gazed inside. At the bottom, twisted and broken, lay the bodies of Simon and the beast in a pool of shallow water and moonlight. Neither moved nor would they ever again.

Gabriel wanted to cry for Simon but couldn't just yet. Maybe in time. He was thankful that Simon was finally free of the beast, though at such an enormous cost. Gabriel sighed and gently caressed Violet's face, indicating to her with melancholy eyes that it was time to leave. They would have much to tell the others when they returned home.

CHAPTER TWENTY

Weather and Time

Gabriel and Violet hurried to the shrubbery on the side of the house. To their dismay, none of their friends were around. Tangled strings of colored lights glared painfully over the lawn. Toppled chairs lay on the ground, some hidden in night shadows, others frozen in the moonlight. The fascinated whispers of partygoers filled the air, with occasional interruptions by Major Grump. The dog continued to bark in his pen, disgruntled that he wasn't allowed to stand at the front gate and watch the excitement.

"Where is everybody?" Violet asked as she and Gabriel observed the scene from beneath the shrubs. "I'm almost afraid to learn what happened while we were at the well."

"We'll find out soon enough when we get home. Some of the others *must* have escaped the beasts," Gabriel said confidently, as if merely wishing for good news would make it so.

Then something happened that caused Gabriel and Violet to shudder in disgust. Two men from the house walked slowly across the lawn towards the front gate. They wore thick garden gloves as they clutched the five dead beasts by their tails. Expressions of rage and defiance were permanently etched on the creatures' bloody faces. The stiffening bodies swayed in the shadows as the men disappeared. Gabriel never learned nor cared to know what finally became of the carcasses.

After exploring a few minutes and finding no one, Gabriel and Violet thought it best to return home. They scurried through the grass to Gabriel's hole under the back shrubbery since it was closer, and their hearts leapt when Florence appeared from behind a small rock to greet them.

"Gabriel and Violet! You're both alive!" she chattered with all the enthusiasm of a younger mouse tasting its first gulp of spring air. "We thought we might never see you again. Everyone, Gabriel and Violet are back!"

When the other mice heard the wonderful news, they rushed out from their hiding spots to greet the couple and cheered that they had escaped the leader of the beasts. A few mice had seen Gabriel and Violet flee from the beast shortly after the initial attack, certain they'd have no chance of surviving. All delighted in how wrong those doubters had been.

"When the trouble ended, everyone agreed to gather in this spot," Florence said. "Since you and Violet were the only mice unaccounted for, we decided it best to wait here by your home, hoping against hope that you'd return. And as glorious as the rising sun, you've both come back safely!" Florence, choked with emotion, wiped away a few tears.

The other mice gathered around Gabriel and Violet, thrilled to see them and eager to learn what had happened to the last beast. Gabriel promised to answer all questions in due time, but only after they filled him in on the details from the party. He and Violet were curious to know what happened after they had fled for their lives.

The crowd went silent. The news was not good. The thrill of seeing Gabriel and Violet alive made the others momentarily forget the traumatic ordeals they had just been through as well. Several took turns explaining events with somber and faltering voices.

Gabriel and Violet were distraught when they learned that seven mice had been killed in the attack. Edmund, sadly, was among the dead, having perished while leading a group of mice to safety. Gabriel recalled first meeting Edmund at the frog pond and how bravely he had led the group of mice to the estate. He would be terribly missed.

"Edmund was such an important member of our community," Toby said in a raspy voice. "I don't know how we'll get by without his leadership."

"Sometimes leadership springs from the most unexpected individuals," Gabriel replied, hoping to comfort his friend. "From what I've seen, Toby, *you* are just as valuable to our society as anyone here. And now more than ever, we'll need your guidance and experience."

The other mice echoed Gabriel's sentiments, but Toby was too flustered by their kind words to respond.

Surprisingly, only three mice sustained any other injuries in the attacks, Chester being one of them. His wound, though, wasn't too deep and would mend quickly. A mouse named Holly, whom Chester had protected during the attack, fussed over him nonetheless. Chester didn't mind the extra attention in the least and chatted with Holly till after the moon had set.

"Now we need to know what happened to you two," Florence insisted. She and the others surrounded Gabriel and Violet till they could barely move their tails. "Tell us at once! How did you escape the beast?"

"And is it still alive?" Elmer piped in.

Violet, sensing anxiety and sadness in Gabriel's eyes, asked the others to step back and give them some room. "Gabriel has just been through a harrowing ordeal. Give him a few moments to rest."

"No, I'm okay," he said, appreciative of Violet's concern. "I *want* to tell everyone what happened, though it won't be easy or pleasant to hear."

The mice looked stunned and horrified as Gabriel outlined Simon's role in the assault. Eyes widened and noses twitched as they learned how Simon had met with the beasts beyond the stone wall. No one could believe that one of their own would consort with the enemy to plan such a dreadful invasion. When Gabriel explained the role Simon had played in Lewis and Jalin's deaths, the mice were dumbfounded. Many couldn't speak for several moments as they tried to make sense of such a traitorous act.

"Why would he turn against us?" Florence meekly asked. "We were his friends. I don't understand how Simon could *do* such a thing."

"Perhaps we'll never know," Gabriel speculated.

He then described his and Violet's final confrontation on top of the well with Simon and the beast. The mice listened in absolute silence and gasped when hearing about the creature's plunge into the murky depths of the well and how Simon was pulled in at the last moment. Relief, however, spread through the group with the knowledge that the leader of the beasts was finally dead. As to Simon's demise, some of the mice felt sadness, others disappointment, and a few nothing at all. Much time would have to pass before any of them could begin to tackle their true feelings about what Simon had done.

"Things may have turned out differently if Simon had been stronger," Gabriel said. "If he had only counted on his friends. Trusted us enough to help him." He sighed, quite exhausted and on the verge of tears. "Let's not discuss Simon anymore tonight. In fact, I don't feel much like talking about *anything* right now. I just want to rest. Simply rest."

Gabriel felt better the next day as the early morning sun warmed his back. The mice were joyful to see the light of day, knowing that the beasts would never bother them again. Gathering in the dewy grass after their morning meal, the mice followed Gabriel to the stone well so he could better explain the events of the previous night.

He described how he and Violet had been chased over the estate grounds, and narrated with dramatic flair their near capture by the pond. But the tale of Gabriel and Violet's final confrontation atop the well proved to be the most enthralling part of the story, one which several mice asked to hear over and over for many days.

Then in small groups, the mice took turns scaling the well to the top to see for themselves the fate of Simon and the beast. Many shuddered when viewing the misshapen bodies sprawled out on the bottom. Most kept silent afterwards, thankful that the curse of the beasts had ended.

"I think this area should be a spot for celebrating from now on," Toby said after the last group returned to the ground. "This is where the evil that invaded our home was destroyed. We should be joyful whenever we're nearby."

"Nonsense!" Florence said gravely. "This area by the well is full of heartbreak and despair and should be approached with no joy whatsoever. Anyone who comes here should think of the woe brought to us by the beasts and mourn for those mice who perished. I'll never celebrate here."

Opinions were mixed regarding Florence and Toby's suggestions. But as the final days of summer slipped away at a frightening speed, most of the mice used the well area simply as a place to think in silence. Most dealt with their loss in private, trying to comprehend the horror, yet looking back fondly on brighter days and wishing for better ones to come. But in a short time, none of the mice went near the well for a while because of a rising lingering stench from the decaying bodies.

Though never forgotten, the events surrounding Simon and the beast were pushed to the back of everyone's mind as autumn rolled around. The leaves on the trees erupted in shades of orange, gold and red as the mice busied themselves with storing food for the winter and preparing warm bedding in their holes. There wasn't much time to contemplate the events of summer.

When finally the first winter snow fell and icy winds blew fiercely across the estate grounds, the mice's only concern was to keep warm in the depths of their dark holes and enjoy a long restful sleep. The good days and the bad of last summer now drifted into the realm of distant memory to be sorted out another time.

But as each day slipped into the next, collecting into pools of weeks and months, the sun started climbing higher in the sky. The winds warmed the frozen ground, and creaky pine trees shrugged off remnants of lingering snow from their fragrant boughs. Streams bubbled again to full life in the fields, rising up along their muddy banks. Flowers strained to pop out of the ground, while robins and sparrows returned from the south and busied themselves with building nests. Eventually the mice poked their noses out of the ground to test the cool fresh earthy air as blankets of white transformed into patches of green. By mid-April, spring had more or less arrived.

The mice were elated to run around the estate grounds again. They explored the rock gardens and frog pond as if seeing them for the first time. Many tumbled in the plush grass under the sweet air and the warm sun, filling up on the fresh food of the new season and thrilled to be alive.

Not until late May when routines had been well established again, did the mice talk about the events of last summer at length. Curiosity about the well grew quickly, so an expedition was organized one afternoon for those wanting another look. Gabriel and Violet were unanimously chosen to lead the way, and were awarded the honor—or chore, depending on one's frame of mind—to climb to the top of the well and have the first glance.

"I feel duty bound to look first, Violet. The others expect it of me, I think," Gabriel said after he and Violet climbed to the top. The hot sun warmed the slate rim.

"Many of them think highly of you, Gabriel. You've earned their respect," she proudly said. "But let's do this together," Violet added with a reassuring smile.

"All right," he said, smiling back.

They walked slowly to the inside edge of the well and looked down. As their eyes adjusted to the darkness, they saw their reflections below in a foot of icy crystal-clear water left behind from the melted snow. Underneath the water were a few sharp rocks, upon which lay two glistening white skeletons, one much larger than the other. The bones remained still, as if encased in glass, yet were set at awkward angles in a testament to their final plunge.

As the well water evaporated through the spring and summer months, the bones dried and fell apart. Some of the smaller ones crumbled to dust. Heavy mid-summer rains further destroyed the remains, and by August, none of the mice who again dared to look inside the well could even tell that the two bodies had ever been down there in the first place. All physical traces of last summer's trouble vanished as gently as night conceding to the dawn.

CHAPTER TWENTY-ONE

Another Journey

The latter days of summer drifted by warm and breezy as August gently faded into September. Lush green tree leaves and a rainbow array of wildflowers offered no hint of an impending autumn. Life at the estate proved enjoyable for the mice, except for Gabriel, who battled bouts of melancholy despite the exceptional weather. Violet guessed that memories of Simon and the events of last summer still haunted him, and she hoped Gabriel would snap out of his doldrums before cooler days arrived.

That wasn't to be. Gabriel acted sociably with his friends and joined them to forage or participate in games near the pond. Yet Violet and the others noticed a peculiar restlessness had overcome him, causing Gabriel many times to lose his train of thought or to stare blankly beyond the stone wall when he thought nobody was around. Even when Gabriel seemed to be in high spirits, some detected a lingering sadness deep in his eyes. Others reasoned he might merely be homesick, but Violet convinced herself that there was something else to it.

"I worry about him more and more each day," she confided to Chester and Elmer amidst a clump of clover near the side wall. "Gabriel hasn't enjoyed a peaceful life since we arrived here. I *know* something's bothering him, but he always puts up a front."

"He misses the freedom and openness of the field," Chester said. "I miss it too. Gabriel isn't happy here, but I don't think he'd ever be satisfied being back home either. There are too many bad memories in both places."

Violet agreed.

"Of course Gabriel would never admit having these feelings," Elmer added. "He's very fond of you, Violet, and wouldn't want to upset your life here. But he'll settle in nicely as the seasons advance, and when the past doesn't loom so large in his mind. Give him time."

"I suppose that's all I *can* do," Violet said. She sighed, and then offered her friends a smile for their time before scurrying through the grass back home.

The uncertainty about Gabriel's condition was temporarily set aside a few days later when Orville came swooping over the wall and settled down among the mice late one afternoon. No one had seen the blackbird since early spring when he had stopped by once to check on how the mice had survived their first winter at the estate.

"Orville!" Gabriel cried with delight, fondly remembering old times. "It's good to see you again. What brings you here?"

"And what news do you have from the field?" Florence asked as she scrambled towards him.

Orville greeted the excited mice with a sweeping scan of his dark eyes, his head bobbing as he paced a few steps before settling down. "I've come here for two reasons," he said.

"First tell us how everyone is back home," someone eagerly called out just as Orville was about to speak.

Orville refrained from snapping back, as he usually would have done when being interrupted. "Your friends are carrying on nicely now that the beasts have been defeated. There was much celebration this past spring, and the young mice who wanted to journey here last year now see no reason to do so."

"Maybe we can meet them halfway next spring and celebrate together for a few days in the field," Holly suggested.

"Perhaps," Orville said flatly.

Gabriel noticed that Orville's usual air of self-importance seemed to be missing this visit, and he quietly mentioned this fact to Violet. Something was definitely bothering their friend.

"What did you want to tell us?" Gabriel asked cautiously.

"I have some unhappy news that I have been requested to relay to you," he said. Orville tucked in his sleek black wings and stood tall and proud. "I've been given the unhappy task to report that old Thackery mouse has passed away. He died two days ago."

The mice were stunned and saddened by the news, offering solace to one another by recalling the many wise words that Thackery had bestowed upon them. He had been a constant in their lives, just like the trees, the sun and the grass. The loss was monumental and full of pain.

"Just before he died, Thackery expressed his thanks to the mice back home for all the kindness and respect shown to him throughout his life," Orville continued. "The last time I spoke to him he asked that I offer all of you his warmest wishes should I ever fly this way again. And I do so now."

The mice thanked Orville many times over for honoring old Thackery's request. Some thought that the bird was quite saddened by the loss, though he would never admit it. But after much reminiscing about Thackery, Orville squawked before announcing his second bit of news.

"What is it?" Florence piped up as Orville returned to his old impatient self.

"I have a second communication, remember? Or more precisely, a *presentation*," he said. This description intrigued the mice and quieted them down. Orville again commanded the crowd which pleased him greatly. "I bring you a surprise."

Orville walked over to Toby and whispered a few words into his ear, causing the mouse to dash to the stone wall while taking a pair of helpers with him. Orville, in the meantime, instructed the other mice to follow him to the wall where the surprise would be revealed.

The mice accompanied him through the grass under the pale golden light of the sinking sun. Wisps of red and purple clouds nuzzled close to the western horizon. All wondered what Orville's surprise might be, but were unsuccessful getting even the slightest hint out of him. Upon arriving at the wall, Gabriel saw that Toby and his helpers had already removed the small stones from the secret passage.

"What's going on?" Violet inquired.

"Do you plan to take us out into the field?" asked Gabriel with a tremor of excitement that Violet clearly noted.

"I have no such intention," Orville replied. "I bring you something even better than a twilight stroll in the outside field." He flapped his wings then pointed his beak at the secret entrance. "Now I present to you two very wonderful and cheerful souls!"

At that instant, Fred and Doris emerged through the hole to the amazement and delight of everyone. Cheers and shouts of joy erupted, and a celebration commenced shortly afterwards at the garden pond when Fred announced that he and Doris were going to stay and live at the estate.

"Fred and I were getting awfully tired of living by the stream. Flooding each spring. Mud everywhere! We're not getting any younger," Doris said. "So if we didn't retire here before the end of this summer, we'd probably never risk the journey. Orville was kind enough to guide us."

Everyone excitedly welcomed their dear old friends into the community. Gabriel eagerly questioned Fred and Doris about his old home well into the night, recalling many fond and cherished memories. He wanted to know every detail about their journey to the estate, envying their adventure. Florence also stayed and chatted with them, elated to have other mice from her generation with her at the estate. Violet excused herself, however, saying she needed to get some rest.

Orville left shortly after daybreak the following morning with an abundance of thanks from the other mice. But just before he departed, Violet engaged him in a long and private conversation near the rock garden. None of the mice who had seen them speaking had any idea what the two discussed, and Violet never gave them the slightest hint.

The last days of September turned chilly and gray, and the surrounding trees shed their leaves like snow. Autumn's first cold snap arrived in early October as dazzling white frost coated the field each morning, graying away the healthy green landscape day by day.

The mice believed that a heavy snowfall couldn't be far behind. Then blessedly, a stretch of Indian summer cloaked the countryside for a brief time, warming the hearts and limbs of the mice, and holding the threat of winter at bay if only for a while.

During this string of delightful days, as the mice gathered food for winter storage and added to the bedding in their holes, Violet privately asked Gabriel to follow her to a spot near the back section of the stone wall. Here a clump of goldenrod grew and few mice lived nearby. The sun gently splashed upon the stones as it peeked through a passing armada of billowy clouds.

"What's going on, Violet? Why are you so secretive this morning?" Gabriel asked.

"I wanted to speak to you about something important," she said quite seriously. "In private."

"You have my undivided attention. What's on your mind?"

"Gabriel, do you like living here?" she bluntly asked. "And be honest with me. I can tell if you're lying."

Gabriel wrinkled his nose as he tugged at his whiskers. "Why are you asking me such a question, Violet? Of course I enjoy living here. And you *love* it from what you've told me. A mouse couldn't ask for anything more."

"But most mice haven't endured what you have recently. I know you try to hide your true feelings, Gabriel—and maybe you're doing so for my sake—but I can see it in your eyes. You're not content living at the estate."

"Violet, that's ridiculous! I—"

"Let me finish, Gabriel. I know we make each other very happy, but we can share that joy *anywhere*." Violet stared into Gabriel's charcoal-black eyes till he could no longer hide his anguish. "Ever since Simon died, this place has held nothing but bad memories for you. And it was never your real home, Gabriel. We only came here to escape the beasts."

"Maybe that's true, Violet, but we'll be all right in time. You'll see."

"Perhaps, but I also think you sorely miss the freedom and vastness of the field. There lies the home you know and love in your heart. You didn't really want to journey to the estate, but you had to for all our sakes." Gabriel wanted to reply, but Violet gently caressed his face and he let her continue. "Still, I don't think you want to return to the old home after what happened to Livingston. Too many bad memories there as well."

"So I guess I'm stuck," Gabriel said with a sigh, trying to smile.

"No, silly. You're not stuck. You simply make a brand new start instead. *We* make a new start—together."

"Violet, what are you saying?"

"What she is *saying* in her roundabout way, Gabriel, is that it's high time you looked for a new home for the two of you."

Gabriel spun around in wide-eyed wonder. There, bobbing casually out from behind the thicket of goldenrod, was Orville, his feathers sleek as night and his attitude as prickly as nettles. He snapped up a bug from the ground while Gabriel scratched his swimming head.

"What are *you* doing here, Orville? And how do you know what Violet was planning?"

"Because, silly mouse, I am her co-conspirator. However, I felt too restless to keep hidden in the goldenrod as requested until she broke the news to you."

Violet giggled at Orville's bristling impatience. "It's true, Gabriel. I recruited Orville to assist me in my little scheme."

"Scheme? Explain please," Gabriel said, standing on his hind legs and gazing suspiciously at Violet and Orville. "What mischief were you two plotting?"

"Please don't get too upset about me going behind your back, Gabriel, but I asked Orville to scout out some new territory in the field. A space that might—well—make a suitable new home for us?"

"And I found the perfect spot," Orville proudly said. "Due north of here, less than half the distance to your old home. Lovely grassy field with gentle hills. A winding stream gurgling nearby. Similar to where you last lived, yet refreshingly different."

"Sounds inviting," Violet said. She stared at Gabriel with an encouraging gleam in her eyes. "So what do you think? Want to check it out?"

Gabriel stood next to Violet and tenderly rubbed his cheek to hers. "You're really willing to leave this place and go back into the wild with me?"

"Of course I am, Gabriel. I'd go anywhere to be with you. I can't imagine life another way."

Gabriel looked at the ground and smiled, so happy to have found Violet. He truly loved her and only now fully realized the depth of *her* love for him. His heart felt as light as clouds.

"In that case, when do we leave?" he asked.

"Orville and I already discussed the particulars," Violet explained. "He has agreed to guide you north so you can find us an appropriate place to live. When all is ready, return for me. In the meantime, I'll say my goodbyes here."

"You two sneaks have every detail figured out," Gabriel said with a grin. "So, you wish to be my guide, Orville? I'm afraid I'll be an awfully slow traveler compared to what you're used to when flying with your friends."

"I learned that distressing fact when I guided Fred and Doris to this place. If only *everybody* had wings," Orville said with a disappointed sigh. "But you need not worry about being a burden to me, Gabriel. I won't be your guide after all." Orville noticed that Violet's carefree countenance turned sour, so he quickly walked over to her. "This is the point where I must confess a deception of my own, Violet. I, too, have conspired with others to help make this little surprise of yours possible."

"What do you mean, Orville?"

"I can't spend these precious few days of autumn exploring the countryside with mice when I have a family of my own to attend to," he said. "However, I took the liberty of providing Gabriel with two quite capable companions to help him scout out the new territory."

Then Orville indicated a small rock nearby surrounded with dry brittle grass. He squawked once and suddenly Chester and Elmer emerged from behind the stone and joined the group. Gabriel and Violet looked equally surprised.

"And who *else* knows about our secret plans?" Violet asked Orville, only pretending to be upset.

"Well if *these* two know," Gabriel said, pointing to Chester and Elmer, "then there's no telling how many others will soon find out."

"Rest assured," Chester replied. "We told no one about your impending journey. No one needs to know until you plan to leave here for good."

"Not a soul," Elmer concurred. "Besides, why would we want to raise all sorts of fuss when *we* plan to travel with you? We're not only going to keep you company on the journey, Gabriel, but we're going to find new homes out in the wild as well. I've begun to miss the field lately and a change of scenery would do me good."

"Me too," Chester said. "I promised Holly—"

"You told *Holly*?"

"Well of course, Gabriel. After I find a place to live, I'll return for her when you come back for Violet. She was so excited about returning to the field too."

"It'll be nice to have her along for company," Violet said.

Gabriel was pleased that their friends would be traveling with them. "I shouldn't expect news like this to remain secret too long in such a close-knit community. Though I'm curious how many other mice will find out before we actually leave," he said with a chuckle.

"At least *one* more mouse!" a peppery voice said. At once, Florence bounded onto the scene, her skinny body as fidgety as a leaf in a whirlwind. "So everybody was just going to disappear as quickly as a dragonfly without saying goodbye to *me*?" she said, feigning hurt feelings.

"They're not leaving for good just yet," Orville assured her. "But how, may I ask, Florence, did *you* find out?"

"I had my suspicions that something was afoot, what with so many mice sneaking off to the back wall. And I noticed you, Orville, alighting on a nearby tree branch earlier *without* announcing your presence in your usual grand style. That itself was worth an investigation. Oh yes," Florence added with a satisfied glint in her eyes. "You don't get to be my age without noticing a thing or two. All I did was put the pieces together."

So Orville and the five mice discussed the details of their plans without any further disruptions that morning. Orville provided Gabriel with a precise layout of the terrain to the north and assured him that the journey should be safe and pleasantly uneventful.

"Nothing as horrible as last year's trip, I'm sure."

"We'll return in a few days to pick you and Holly up," Gabriel said to Violet. "I suspect by then that the others will notice we're missing and start to ask questions. So no use in hiding the truth. Instead, you might suggest holding a celebration at the frog pond on our final night here. We can tell stories and feast for an entire day if we'd like."

"Sounds like a wonderful idea!" Violet said. "Florence, Holly and I will make the preparations while you're gone. Orville, I expect you and Wilbur to make a brief appearance at our final gathering."

"I'll see if I can fit it into my schedule," he said, pretending to be bothered, though knowing he wouldn't miss the festivities for anything. Shortly after, Orville fluttered off, leaving the mice to sort out the details. A string of exuberant squawks punctuated his flight as the blackbird disappeared against the brilliant blue canopy of morning.

That night, when a million fire-white stars dotted the icy black sky, Gabriel and Violet returned to the stone wall near the secret entrance. Chester and Elmer, along with Holly and Florence, accompanied them, as well as Toby, who was finally let in on the secret. In no time the small stones were removed from the wall and the seven mice scurried into the field. A thin crescent moon dangled low above the western horizon.

"Now you be careful, Gabriel. I want you back here as soon as can be," Violet said with a heavy heart. She felt as if the next few days would last a lifetime.

"That goes for you too, Chester," Holly added with a quiver in her voice. "I miss you already."

"I promise to keep a sharp eye on them both," Elmer promised.

Gabriel flashed a reassuring smile at Violet. "We'll be fine and back here before you know it. Trust me," he whispered as he gently nuzzled her nose.

"I do," she whispered back.

"Head straight to the north just like Orville instructed," Florence reminded them. "And make sure you find the best places to live. Violet and Holly deserve firstrate accommodations," she said, raising one of her fingers in mock warning.

"We promise," Gabriel said.

"Good luck," added Toby. "We'll keep a constant lookout for your return."

"Thanks for all your help," he replied.

Then after saying their final goodbyes, Gabriel turned to Chester and Elmer as the chill of night nipped at their ears. "Shall we begin?"

"I'm as ready as I'll ever be," Chester said.

"Me too," Elmer replied with a flick of his tail.

"Then let's go," Gabriel said, looking forward to scampering through the field under a blanket of autumn stars. They planned to head straight for the willow tree, and then continue north into unexplored territory. Gabriel felt a rush of excitement sweep over him. He couldn't help remembering similar journeys with Simon and Livingston and was so glad to be out in the wild again. He waved goodbye to Violet one more time before the trio marched forward into the night.

"How long do you think it'll take us to get there?" Chester asked.

"And when do we stop for our first meal?" Elmer eagerly added.

Gabriel laughed to himself and hurried on like a fleeting breeze. "The only thing I know for sure is that there's a long road ahead," he said to his companions. "And I'm looking forward to every step of the way!"

THE END

ABOUT THE AUTHOR

Thomas J. Prestopnik is a graduate of the State University of New York at Oswego, where he studied in the English/Writing Arts program. *Gabriel's Journey* is his second published novel. He is currently working on the first of two sequels to his debut novel *The Visitors In Mrs. Halloway's Barn*, another children's fantasy-adventure. The title of the sequel will be *The Sword and the Crown*. He resides and writes in Little Falls, NY.

Printed in the United States
PP71100003B